i

Defensive Shotgun – 2nd Edition
Mastering the Versatility
Tactics for Repelling a Deadly Encounter
by Mark "Six" James

Copyright © 2012 by Samurai Publishing

ISBN 978–0–615–60799-3

Published by Samurai Publishing
3695F Cascade Road
Suite 2207
Atlanta, GA 30331
(404) 349-9117

Direct inquires and/or orders to the above address.

You and only you are responsible for your actions. The information contained in this book is designed to help you increase your knowledge in safe firearms handling; provide you with a platform in which to build your shooting skills and provide you some practical defensive techniques.

The use of force laws and this book should under no circumstances to be viewed as a restatement of the law in any jurisdiction or to assure compliance with any applicable federal, state or local laws, ordinances, rules or regulations. You must consult a local attorney to ascertain compliance with all applicable federal, state or local laws, ordinances rules or regulations.

Firearms, shooting, and training are potentially dangerous and can lead to serious injury or death. Discharging firearms in poorly ventilated areas, cleaning firearms, or handling lead or lead containing reloading components may result in exposure to lead. Wash hands after handling ammunition or discharging your firearm.

Each and every person involved in firearms training should act as a safety officer and be constantly alert to any potential safety violations. Care and safe handling is essential.

By receiving and/or reviewing this book, subsequent classroom or range training you agree to not hold the author, instructors, trainers, publishers or company liable for its contents and your subsequent use of the materials or techniques discussed. You hereby release the author, instructors, trainers, publishers and company harmless and release them from liabilities, any cause of action, civil or criminal, which may result due to the use or misuse negligence, misconduct, of the course materials and its instructions.

Firearms Liability

This book is designed for the readers and students of our instructional training sessions to understand some critical firearms liability areas.

Straw Buyers – straw buyers are people who make firearms purchases for people who are not authorized to buy a firearm. Care should be taken when considering purchasing a firearm for someone else or when selling a firearm. That is why many states limit private firearms sales and require sales to be made through firearms dealers. That allows further scrutiny by officials, particularly when that gun is sold on consignment or by the respective consignment dealer. Selling your firearm though a dealer helps reduce your potential exposure and liability.

Discharging your firearm – we should all understand when we discharge our firearms we are responsible for those rounds until they stop (and even after that). That is why constant training, care and discretion should be used whenever we take a shot. Every round that misses your target puts yourself and others at risk. Always know what is behind and around your target.

Lost or stolen firearms – should be reported to the police and your insurance company immediately. A copy of that report and record should be kept for your own protection.

Kids – all firearms should be stored away from kids. You should take advantage of as many countermeasures as possible to protect children. Unloading all firearms, separating weapons from ammunition, applying gun locks to firearms, and placing firearms in a gun safe are basic countermeasures.

TABLE OF CONTENTS

Chapter 7 - Engaging the Threat   137

Chapter 8 – One Hand Operation   189

Author's Message

This book is written for anyone who understands that the lives of people we love can be irretrievably broken by a home invasion or other deadly force encounter. While many law abiding citizens insure their property, the protection of life against deadly force encounters is often ignored. The probability of becoming the victim of a home invasion or personal assault far outweighs the chances of becoming the victim of a fire. Yet, many people understand their options for protecting against fire better than they comprehend their alternatives for protecting life.

As a professional who spends nearly every waking hour focused on protecting life or training others to protect life, I have written this book to present the modern shotgun as a viable defense option for personal safety. This book helps crack the code around the mystery, mystique and often miscommunication about the modern shotgun. It presents tactical applications written so the average citizen or trained operator can understand how to maximize the effectiveness of this incredible tool.

The protection of one's life or the life of a loved one is a mindset. The mindset begins with awareness of how quickly one can become a victim of a deadly encounter, and how readily you can prepare to guard against the most dire outcome once awareness becomes part of your daily reality. The modern shotgun is a tool to help you accomplish your personal, team or agency's safety mission. After reading this book and practicing the recommended tactics, you will improve your situational awareness and, with training, you will significantly enhance your ability to protect life in the event of a deadly encounter.

Please enjoy the reading and make time to master the techniques at the range. Stay aware, stay focused and stay safe; and may God continue to bless and watch over you and your families.

Special thanks to Carla, Chris, Darryl, Darion, Donna, Julie, Lana, Mike, Mike, Mitch, Renee, Russ and Walt for your support.

Cover photo by Russ Bryant.

From "On Combat" Dave Grossman and Loren W. Christensen

"Who ultimately makes the decision that deadly force is needed? The suspect does. The enemy does. The threat does. He fights, you fight. When he uses deadly force, you use deadly force. He has the option to surrender, and your job is to respond with what society says is your right and responsibility to do.

This is the greatest paradox of combat: If you are truly prepared to kill someone, you are less likely to have to do it."

Chapter 1

Getting Started

"A Shotgun must have three things
Boom, Boom, Boom"
Phil Robertson, Benelli Pro

Getting Started

Basic Firearm Safety

- Treat all guns as if they are always loaded. Even when you just unloaded them, treat them as if they're loaded.
- Never point the muzzle at anything you aren't willing to destroy!
- Keep your finger off the trigger except when ready to shoot.
- Watch what is in the background of your target in case you miss. What is going to stop the shot or slug if/and when you fire?

Firearm Range Safety

- No alcohol allowed at the range or prior to coming to the range.
- Eye and ear protection should be worn at all times.
- Weapons should be unloaded prior to entering the range.
- No loaded weapons are allowed in the classroom or any other place at the range except on the firing line.
- Load weapon only on command (cold range).
- All weapons must always be pointed down-range (the direction of the targets) at all times.
- When not on the firing line, all weapons should have the action visibly open.
- NEVER point your weapon anywhere other than at the ground and the target/backstop/butts/pits (all different terms for where the targets are).
- Keep your finger off the trigger except when ready to fire.

Getting Started

- Shoot only at the assigned targets.
- No dry firing allowed behind the firing line.
- Never move forward of the firing line for any reason. If you drop anything forward of the line notify your range officer.
- If your weapon jams, fails to fire or misfires, place it on the range bench rest pointing down range and contact your range officer.
- No horseplay is allowed on the range.

Common Range Terms

- Hot Range – a range where guns are expected to be loaded all the time without commands to "reload" by the range officer.
- Cold Range – a range where guns are unloaded most of the time and only loaded and reloaded by the direction of the range officer.
- Danger Zone – anything in front of the line of fire or where you must keep your weapon pointed whenever it is un-holstered, un-slung or mounted.
- Safe Zone – is everything behind the line of fire. This is where you want to keep all of your body parts. You should avoid having your weapon un-holstered, un-slung, mounted or pointed in the safe zone.

Getting Started

Things to know as you prepare to train

Where do you want to concentrate your training?

- More than 80% of gunfights occur within the 7 yard distance.
- Over half of those happened within 5 feet or less!
- 15% of fights occur at distances exceeding 50 feet.
- Gunfights tend to be sudden and violent. The estimated elapsed time is roughly 3 seconds.
- About 70% of gunfights occur in reduced light environments.
- Almost 50% of the time you might face more than one assailant.
- Most shotgun encounters tend to be pretty conclusive, and are typically over in 2 shots or less.

In its traditional use the shotgun is often utilized at handgun distances to give the user a significantly more powerful edge, often with enhanced margin for error.

Getting Started

Understanding your Shotgun

Why we own Shotguns?

There are multiple reasons people purchase shotguns.
Below are the Top 6 reasons consumers purchase shotguns:

- Collecting
- Competitive Shooting
- Duty
- Hunting
- Personal Protection
- Recreational Shooting

Getting Started

Selecting a Shotgun

Things to consider when selecting a shotgun:

- What is the intended purpose of the shotgun?
- Will it be primarily used for home protection, sporting or as a duty weapon?
- If this is a duty weapon are there specific departmental considerations I must take into account (i.e. pump action only)?
- Who else in my household may use this weapon?
- Among those of us who will use the shotgun, how much time will we devote to training?
- Is the gauge appropriate for my intended application?
- Do I need a barrel with rifling for enhanced accuracy?
- Do I need a cylinder bore to accommodate a wider variety of loads?
- Would my family's or my personal needs be better satisfied through multiple shotgun purchases, as opposed to one size fits all?

Getting Started

Basic Shotgun parts and descriptions

- Action Release
- Bore
- Butt Stock
- Cast
- Comb
- Forearm
- Heel
- Length of Pull
- Line of Sight
- Magazine
- Porting
- Ribline
- Toe
- Trigger
- Trigger Guard
- Wrist

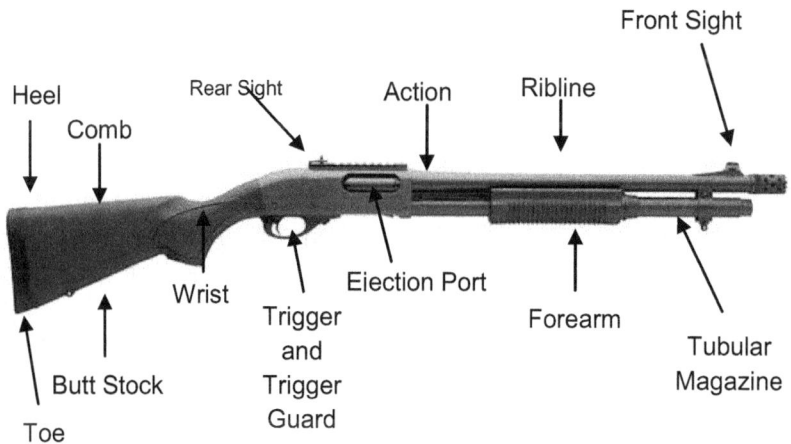

Front Sight

Heel
Comb
Rear Sight
Action
Ribline

Wrist
Ejection Port
Trigger
and
Trigger
Guard
Forearm

Butt Stock
Tubular
Magazine

Toe

Getting Started

Common Definitions

- Action – the mechanism of a firearm by which it is loaded locked, fired and unloaded.
- Action Release – is the method by which the action is closed or opened.
- Bore – hole in the barrel through which the shot passes.
- Breakpoint – point at which the target is expected to be broken without rushing the shot. This is a term usually utilized in skeet or trap shooting.
- Butt Stock – the portion of the stock behind the receiver/action. This is the part that comes into contact with the shoulder.
- Cast – the distance the stock angles left (cast on) or right (cast off) from the receiver when viewed from the rear (this allows for easier horizontal alignment of the dominant eye, with the rib without undue tilting of the head.
- Choke – the decrease in diameter of the bore near the end of the barrel; they are designed to keep a pattern from expanding as quickly at all yardages.
- Comb – the top surface of the stock on which the cheek is placed, either parallel with the barrel or upward-sloping most of the time.
- Fore-end (forearm) – the wood/synthetic grip attached to the barrel in front of the action or receiver.
- Heel – the upper surface of the recoil pad or butt plate (the top of butt) and the second drop dimension given for straight stocks.

Getting Started

- Length of Pull – the distance from the front center of the trigger curvature back to the vertical center of the recoil pad (typically over 14" on most stocks).
- Line of Sight/Sight Line – an imaginary line from the pupil of the eye to the front bead.
- Magazine – is the compartment where the shotgun shells are stored in the shotgun, and may be box or tubular shaped.
- Pattern – the distribution and quantity of shot within or on a target 30 inch circle, from a shell commonly fired from a particular distance. For sport shooters that distance is typically measured at 40 yards and within a 30 inch circle. For defensive or tactical shooting it is whatever distance you desire to measure the maximum effectiveness of.
- Plug – a device used to restrict the amount of ammunition the shotgun can hold.
- Porting – a break or concentration of holes through which gas escapes in the top half of the barrel near the center or more commonly the end. The escaping gases help reduce recoil, but often make the firearm noisier.
- Ribline – the line along the top barrel that extends rearward over the heel from which drop at the comb is measured.
- Toe – Bottom of the butt or recoil pad opposite the heel.
- Wrist – the section of the stock forward of the nose of the comb.

Getting Started

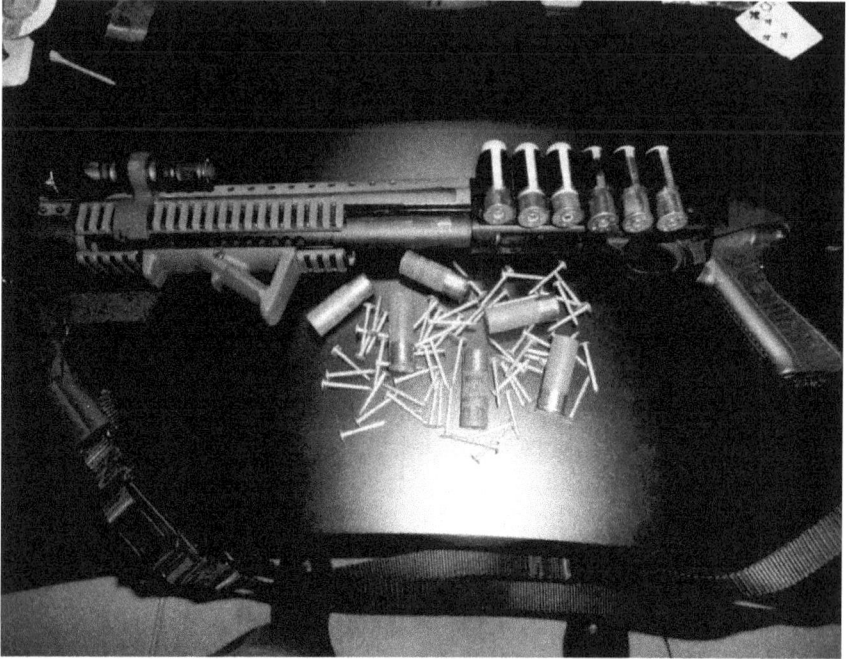

A firearm is just an inanimate piece of metal. You can use it as a paper weight or a hammer. But if you want to use it as an efficient self-defense tool you have to train with it as such.

Chapter 2
Types of Shotguns

I'll take that one please!

Types of Shotguns

Types of Shotguns

- Pumps (Slide Action)
- Automatic (Self Loader)
- Over and Under
- Double Barrel (Side by Side)
- Police or Tactical

While all of the above shotguns provide defensive options it is important to realize the shotgun is just a tool in your list of countermeasures. When it comes to practical defense the best shotgun you have is the one you currently have. As we review various shotguns, the selection of a new shotgun should be based on your specific needs.

Types of Shotguns

If you are considering acquiring a new shotgun the below chart will provide you some general financial considerations:

- $100 - $200 on a hinge action single shot
- $200 - $600 on a pump-action shotgun
- $500 - $1,200 on a semi-auto shotgun
- $1,200 plus for an advanced semi-automatic tactical gun or medium to high-end sporting double-barreled shotgun

Shotguns will range in gauge from 10, 12, 16, 20, 28, and 410. However my recommendation for personal defense or duty is 12 gauge as it gives you the greatest variety of accessory and load options. Followed by 20 gauge for those looking for reduced recoil, although there are a variety of recoil friendly loads available for the 12 gauge. I would consider barrel lengths in the 18 – 22 inch range based on need.

Pump Shotguns

Pump Action – gets its name because the shooter pumps the movable fore-end/forearm back and forth in order to open and close the action. The pumping action empties the chamber and loads a new cartridge or shot-shell from the tubular magazine. It is easy to work for both right and left hand shooters.

Types of Shotguns

Benelli Nova Pump Tactical

The Nova Pump Tactical is a 12-gauge pump-action shotgun that integrates a polymer stock and lightweight receiver into a single unit for unsurpassed strength and weather resistance. High-tech ergonomics make the gun comfortable to hold and easy to handle. Distinctive grooves on the pistol grip and forearm, in place of conventional checkering, provides a positive gripping surface and complements the innovative engineering of the Nova Tactical. Dual-action bars and rotary head locking lugs, allows the Nova Tactical to handle everything from light loads to 3-1/2" magnums. A magazine cut-off on the forearm allows for safe carry with a full magazine and empty chamber.

The Nova Pump Tactical is available with either rifle sights, or a click-adjustable military-style ghost-ring for this all-business, no-nonsense defense tool.

Types of Shotguns

The Nova H2O Pump Tactical utilizes a polymer stock and open rifle sights. The barrel is made of corrosion-resistant stainless steel, magazine tube and cap, trigger group and is nickel plated to insure it keeps working in even the harshest conditions. Available in Black Synthetic the Benelli Nova Pump Tactical is one of the most versatile pump-action shotguns ever made.

Key Features:

- Magazine Capacity: 4 + 1
- Chokes: Improved Cylinder, Modified and Full
- Type of Sights: Open Rifle or Ghost ring; receiver is drilled and tapped for scope mount; Picatinny rail is included
- Barrel length 18 ½ inches
- Overall length 40 inches
- Weight 7.2 lbs
- Length of Pull: 14 3/8 " Drop at Heel 2 ¼" Drop at Comb: 1 ¼"

Types of Shotguns

Benelli Supernova Tactical Pistol Defense

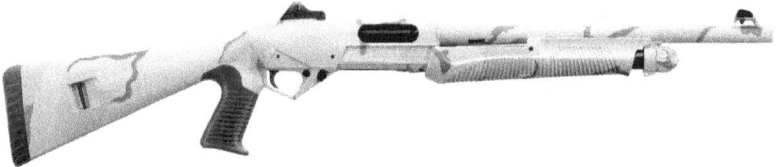

The SuperNova embodies a modular design concept in a pump action shotgun, fitted with a ghost-ring rear sight and pistol grip.

At the heart of this pump gun is a lightweight steel skeleton framework over-molded with a high-tech polymer, making the SuperNova lightweight, super-strong and almost completely impervious to any weather condition. With its dual-action bars and two-lug rotary bolt head that lock up steel to steel inside the barrel, the SuperNova is solid to the core.

Types of Shotguns

Key Features:

- Magazine Capacity: 4 + 1
- Chokes: Cylinder
- Type of Sights: Ghost ring; receiver is drilled and tapped for scope mount; Picatinny rail is included
- Barrel length 18 ½ inches
- Overall length 40 inches
- Weight 7.8 lbs
- Length of Pull: 14 3/8 " Drop at Heel 2 ¼" Drop at Comb: 1 1/2"

Types of Shotguns

Mossberg 590A1

Mossberg 590A1 is a time tested and true battle shotgun. Similar to the Remington 870 it has been the choice for Law Enforcement and Military around the country and around the world. It features a heavy-walled parkerized barrel, metal trigger guard assembly, metal safety button, and an upgraded magazine tube that can easily be opened for cleaning and is readily adaptable for a magazine extension. Its 3 inch chamber will receive either 2 ¾ or 3 inch shells. It comes equipped with an anti-jam elevator, dual extractors for reliable feeding, and positive shot shell extraction and ejection.

Types of Shotguns

590 A1 Blackwater Series

590 A1 Mariner

590 A1 Adjustable

Types of Shotguns

Key Features:

- Stock choices include a 6-position adjustable tactical stock, pistol-grip Cruiser® models, standard full-size polymer stock, or a polymer Speedfeed® model that holds four additional shells in the stock for quick and easy reloading.
- Every 590A1 Special Purpose model features a drilled and tapped receiver, factory-ready for Picatinny rail, scope base or optics installation.
- Overall length 36 1/8 to 41inches, Weight 6 ¾ lbs to 7 1/2 lbs.
- Barrels lengths include 18-1/2" (with 5+1 magazine capacity) or 20" (with 8+1 magazine capacity), all with cylinder bore.
- Depending on the model, you'll find a choice of 3-Dot, Ghost Ring™, or basic front bead sights.
- The deluxe-equipped 590A1™ SPX™ model comes fully loaded out of the box with the features you want: a factory-mounted Picatinny rail, LPA/M16-Style Ghost Ring combination sight set, and removable M9 bayonet/scabbard combination.
- Other 590A1 versions include the 590A1 Mariner® model with Marinecote™-finished barrel and receiver for added corrosion resistance for marine applications, extreme wet weather or humid environments and a reduced (13") length-of-pull 590A1™ Compact model perfect for smaller-stature shooters.
- 590A1 shotguns are also available in 14" Class III Restricted models for law enforcement and military personnel.

Types of Shotguns

Remington 870 Tactical

For many years Remington tactical shotguns have been the gold standard for military and law enforcement operators throughout the world. The Model 870™ express Tactical attempts to continue to build on that legacy with a durable "hammered" gun-metal-grey powder-coat finish, a quick-pointing 18 1/2" barrel and includes an extended ported Tactical Rem Choke. It features a 7 round tubular magazine of 2 3/4" or 3" 12-gauge firepower with the factory installed 2-shot extension.

Types of Shotguns

The Model 870™ express® Tactical with XS® Ghost Ring Sights is designed for rapid target acquisition and precise shot placement with the XS blade sight and XS Ghost Ring sight rail (fully adjustable for windage and elevation), which accepts optics and sight systems as well. Both models have black synthetic stocks and fore-ends with sling swivel studs. Receivers are drilled and tapped.

Key Features:

- 18 1/2" tactical barrel with XS® front blade sight RC Tactical (ext/ported tube)
- XS Ghost Ring sight Rail (mounts to receiver)
- Sight is fully adjustable for windage and elevation
- Front blade sight works in conjunction with Ghost Ring to quickly and accurately acquire target
- Tactical style fore-end
- 2-shot magazine extension
- Receiver drilled and tapped for scope mounts (XS Picatinny rail with ghost ring included)

Types of Shotguns

Remington Express Tactical with Blackhawk Spec Ops II

Key Features:

- 18" tactical barrel with bead sight
- Weight 7 lbs
- Adjustable Stock
- 7 position length of pull adjustment
- Recoil reduction system
- Drilled and tapped receiver
- Fixed Cylinder Choke

Types of Shotguns

Remington 870 Tactical Desert Recon

The Model 870™ Tactical Desert Recon series shotguns are equipped with Tiger Stripe Products® Digital Tiger™ Desert camo stocks and fore-ends, and military-style olive drab powder-coated metalwork. Choose from two different stock designs, 18" or 20" barrels and two- or three-shot magazine-tube extensions. Both come with Remington special ported Tactical Extended Rem™ Choke tube.

Key Features:

- 18" or 20" Tactical Barrel
- Overall Length 38 ½ - 40 ½ inches
- Single Bead Sight
- Tactical Style Fore-end
- Desert Camo on Stock and Fore-end
- Special Ported "Tactical" Extended Rem Choke Tube
- 2- or 3-Shot Magazine Extension

Types of Shotguns

Wilson Combat Professional

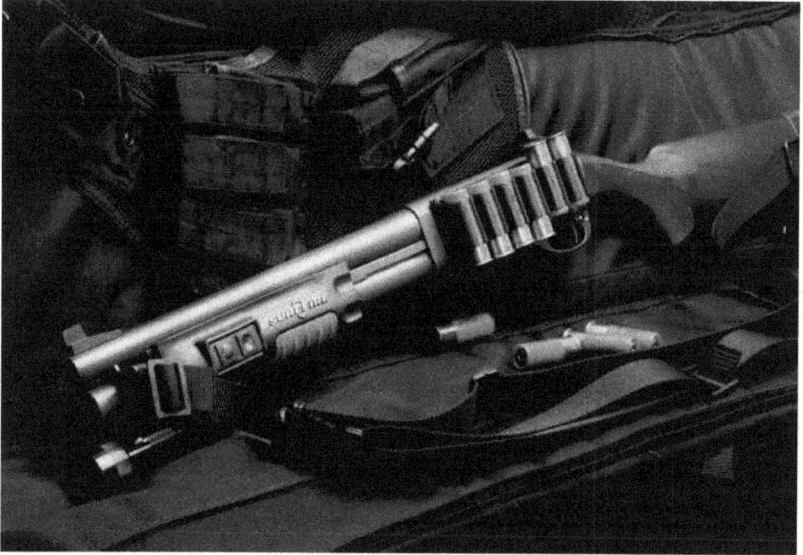

The Professional Model is built exclusively for military and law enforcement professionals. It incorporates the features demanded most in their defensive shotguns: a 14" cylinder-bore barrel with 3" magnum chamber that will handle the ammunition your mission demands – and the included magazine extension tube offers increased capacity for a total of 6 rounds.

Types of Shotguns

It includes an extra-power heavy-duty stainless magazine spring for sure shell feeding in any situation, and a high-visibility, non-binding follower to indicate an empty-magazine tube at a glance. The Professional Model also includes your choice of a four or six round receiver-mounted Sidesaddle shell carrier. – In a critical re-load situation your extra ammo is quickly available in a no fumbling, load-by-feel manner.

The Professional Model is fitted with synthetic butt stock and fore-grip. The fore-grip includes a 6-volt SureFire Tactical Light with 11,000 candlepower – more than enough to assess and react to a combat situation regardless of darkness. Wilson features a variety of buttstock configurations from standard buttstock length, an optional shorter buttstock, Knoxx SpecOps Stock or AR collapsible stock.

Other included features include a Jumbo-head safety, multi-purpose tactical sling, buttstock sling swivel and a rigid magazine tube front sling mount. Our adjustable TRAK-LOCK® Ghost Ring rear sight is paired with a ramp-type front sight with a tritium self-luminous insert for fast and accurate aiming.

Other included features include a Jumbo-head safety, multi-purpose tactical sling, buttstock sling swivel and a rigid magazine tube front sling mount. Adjustable TRAK-LOCK® Ghost Ring rear sight is paired with a ramp-type front sight with a tritium self-luminous insert for fast and accurate aiming.

Types of Shotguns

Key Features:

- Action Pump Caliber 12 Ga. Barrel 14 inches (cylinder bore) Overall Length –Fixed Stock 34.4 inches
- Overall Length –Collapsible Stock Extended 35.3 inches Overall Length
- Collapsible Stock Closed 31.4 inches
- Weight Empty 8.4 lbs
- Capacity 5 +1 Rounds

Types of Shotguns

Kel-Tec KSG Shotgun

The KSG is a bull-pup shotgun design that has two magazine feed tubes, each side capable of holding 7 shells, for a total capacity of 14 +1. The KSG ejects downward, instead of forward. The KSG weighs 6.9lbs and is as compact as legally possible with a 26.1" overall length and an 18.5" cylinder bore barrel. Even with this compact size, the internal dual tube magazines hold an impressive 14 rounds of 12 gage 2-3/4" rounds (7 per tube).

The simple pump action feeds from either the left or right tube. The feed side is manually selected by a lever located behind the trigger guard. The lever can be positioned in the center detent in order to easily clear the chamber without feeding another round from either magazine.

A cross bolt style safety blocks the sear, and the pump release lever is located in front of the trigger guard.

Types of Shotguns

The pump includes an under Picatinny rail for the mounting of a forward grip, or a light or laser. The included top Picatinny sight rail will accept many types of optics or iron sights. Forward and rear sling loops are built in, and a basic sling is included. The soft rubber butt pad helps to tame recoil.

Key Features:

- Action Pump Caliber 12 Ga. Barrel 18.5 inches (cylinder bore)
- Bull-pup Design
- Overall Length – 26.1 inches Overall Length
- Weight Empty 8.4 lbs
- Capacity 14 +1 Rounds

Types of Shotguns

Over & Under and Double Barrel Shotguns

Over & Under and Double Barreled – are sometimes referred to as hinge action shotguns as the shotgun breaks in the center, similar to the movement of a hinge door. Hinge action shotguns do not have magazines and are classified as single-shot firearms. The action is easy to work for both right and left hand shooters.

To open the hinge action, locate the action release levers on the top of the grip stock. Push the action release to one side and move the barrel or barrels downward. If the firearm is loaded the action should automatically eject the ammunition on most models.

While hinge action and other sporting shotguns offer a level of personal protection for home defense, their traditional limited capacity significantly reduce your ability to maintain

Types of Shotguns

continuity of fire, particularly when dealing with multiple adversaries.

Automatics or Self Loaders – are either gas operated or recoil operated. Gas operated means that some of the pressure from the fired cartridge is tapped off the barrel and pushes a piston backwards causing the action to open. It is important to keep semi-automatic firearms clean and use proper ammunition. Semi-automatic weapons often allow the operator to fire follow up shots quicker with minimal need to move the weapon off target.

To prove a semi-automatic firearm is unloaded, it is important to remove the source of ammunition. If the firearm has a magazine remove it, this ensures that only one round will be in the firearm. Operate the cocking lever to eject the ammunition in the chamber. Most automatics have a button or lever to lock the action open. This allows you to observe whether the weapon is empty. Care should be used when checking and avoid putting your finger in the action area. If the action accidentally closes you might injure or sever your finger.

Types of Shotguns

Benelli M2 – Pistol Grip

Benelli M2 – Comfort Tech

The M2 has been the workhorse of the semi-auto Benelli shotguns. The M2 12-gauge shotgun and 20-gauge shotgun are built around the Inertia Driven bolt mechanism. The Inertia Driven system allows the M2 to digest nearly any 12 gauge cartridge, from 2-3/4" target loads to the heaviest 3" magnums.

Benelli's ComforTec system is designed to reduce felt recoil by up to 48% and cuts muzzle climb by 15%. This puts the shooter back on target up to 69% faster than with any other comparable semi-automatic shotgun.

Types of Shotguns

Key Features:

- Magazine Capacity: 4 + 1
- Chokes: Modified
- Type of Sights: Ghost ring; receiver is drilled and tapped for scope mount; Picatinny rail is included
- Barrel length 18 ½ inches
- Overall length 39 ¾ inches
- Weight 6.7 lbs
- Length of Pull: 14 3/8 inches Drop at Heel 2 ¼ inches
- Drop at Comb: 1 ½ inches

Types of Shotguns

Benelli M4 Tactical

The M4 Tactical 12-gauge auto loading shotgun features Benelli's unique Auto Regulating Gas Operated (A.R.G.O.) system. It has dual stainless steel, self-cleaning pistons located just ahead of the chamber that operate directly against the bolt assembly. The M4 Tactical comes standard with a Picatinny rail for optics, a fully adjustable ghost-ring rear sight and fixed-blade front sight and a black synthetic pistol-grip style stock.

Types of Shotguns

M4 Tactical H2O

Key Features:

- Magazine Capacity: 4 + 1
- Chokes: M
- Type of Sights: Ghost ring; receiver is drilled and tapped for scope mount; Picatinny rail is included
- Overall length 40.0"
- Average Weight 7.8 lbs
- Length of Pull: 14 3/8 " Drop at Heel 2 ¼" Drop at Comb: 1 1/2 "

Types of Shotguns

Mossberg 930 SPX

Mossberg 930 Tactical with Heat Shield

The 930 SPX has been considered one of the best values on the market for an auto loader. It was has been named "Shotgun of the Year" by Shooting Illustrated magazine; and was also recognized with the NRA Golden Bullseye Award. For a home defense tool it is simple to operate, dependable firearm in a crisis can make a world of difference. It features a self-regulating gas system, which vents excess gas, to aid in recoil reduction and eliminates stress on critical components.

All 930 autoloaders chamber both 2 3/4 inch and 3-inch 12-gauge shot shells with ease—from target loads, to non-toxic magnum loads, to sabot slug ammo.

Types of Shotguns

Key Features:

- Magazine capacity is 7+1 on models with extended magazine tube, 4+1 on models without. To complete the package, each Mossberg 930 includes a set of specially designed spacers for quick adjustment of the horizontal and vertical angle of the stock, bringing a custom-feel fit to every shooter. Safety and safe handling is of paramount importance in special purpose firearms, and the 930 was engineered with that in mind.
- The receiver-mounted safety is convenient for right or left-handed users; simply push the button forward to take the weapon off safe.
- A protruding chrome cocking-indicator button is strategically placed in the front inner-edge of the trigger guard, making it easy to see and feel when the weapon is cocked or un-cocked.
- Mossberg EZ-Empty™ system. By depressing the bolt release, the carrier can be pushed up and the first shot shell in the magazine removed. Simply repeat until the magazine is empty.
- All 930 Special Purpose models feature a drilled and tapped receiver, factory-ready for Picatinny rail, scope base or optics installation. 930 SPX models conveniently come with a factory-mounted Picatinny rail and LPA/M16-Style Ghost Ring combination sight right out of the box.
- Other sighting options include a basic front bead, or white-dot front sights. Mossberg 930 Special Purpose shotguns are available in a variety of configurations; 5-shot tactical barrel, 5-shot with muzzle brake, 8-shot pistol-grip, and even a 5-shot security/field combo.

Types of Shotguns

Remington Versa Max

The Versa Max is a tactical gas operated auto loading shotgun, featuring a synthetic stock and fore-end. The Versaport gas system regulates cycling pressure based on length of shell. It will handle anything from 2 ¾ inch shells to 3 ½ inch shells. It is customized with a picatinny rail, forward barrel-clamp side rails and an extended magazine.

Types of Shotguns

Key Features:

- Synthetic Stock
- Capacity 8 + 1 Capacity
- Pro Bore Choke system – Improved Cylinder and Tactical Extended
- Average Weight – approximately 8 ¼ pounds
- Average overall length 43 15/16 inches, 22 inch barrel
- Oversized bolt release button and bolt release
- Oversized trigger guard for easy operation with gloves
- Receiver Mounted Picatinny rail
- Picatinny barrel clamp for accessories mounting
- HiViz front sight

Types of Shotguns

Saiga Shotgun

The Saiga 12 gauge is a gas operated semi-automatic shotgun built on the Kalashnikov or AK47 platform. It may be assembled with a fixed or folding stock depending on the shooters preference. While the weapon has been built on a classic AK47 platform there are a number of aftermarket stocks, forearms and accessories available to allow the shooter to customize the weapon to their preferences to be able to accept optics, lights etc. The detachable magazine is preferred by many as it offers shooters a quicker option of getting the shotgun back to full capacity particularly during emergency reloads.

Types of Shotguns

Key Features:

- Semi-Automatic, 5rds
- May be assembled with a Synthetic Stock, Folding Stock, Telescopic or Fixed Stock
- Bolt Stop
- No Choke
- Threaded chrome-lined barrel,
- Adjustable gas system for 2.75" or 3" shells
- Feed System Detachable box magazine – available in 5-round, 10-round, 12-round magazines or 20-round drums.

Types of Shotguns

Police or Tactical Shotguns – may be pump action or semi-automatic. Most are characterized by the shorter barrels usually 18 to 20 inches compared to that of most sporting guns which are often 24, 26, 28, or 30 inch barrels. Most police or tactical shotguns have larger capacity box, clip or tubular magazines.

Types of Shotguns

Commonly Used Tactical Shotguns

Pump Action

- Benelli Supernova Tactical
- Benelli Nova Pump Tactical
- Mossberg 590 with Ghost Rings
- Mossberg 590 with Ghost Rings and Knoxx Spec Ops
- Wilson Combat

Stock

- Mossberg 500 Tactical or Persuader/Cruiser
- Remington 870 TAC-2 with Knoxx Spec Ops Stock
- Remington 870 TAC-2 FS with Spec Ops Folding Stock
- Remington 870 TAC-3 with Speed Feed

Semi-Automatic Shotguns

- Benelli M2 Tactical (Pistol Grip)
- Benelli M2 Tactical (Comfort Tech)
- Benelli M2 Tactical (Standard)
- Benelli M4 Tactical
- Mossberg 930 SPX
- Remington Versa Max Tactical
- Saiga 12 Combat Shotgun

Types of Shotguns

Chapter 3

Understanding Ammunition

Double 00 Buck is what has historically given the shotgun it's bad to the bone reputation.

Understanding Ammunition

Components of a Shotgun Shell

- Shot or Slug – the actual projectile which is expelled from the shotgun.
- Hull – is the actual housing which contains the shot or slug and wad.
- Brass base – the actual housing which contains the gunpowder and primer.
- Gunpowder – any various powders used to expel the projectile from the casing, often made of potassium nitrate, charcoal, and sulfur.
- Wad – the material that the shot or slug sits on. It separates the shot or slug from the powder charge.
- Primer – a cap or a tube containing a small amount of explosive used to ignite the main explosive charge used in a firearm.

Understanding Ammunition

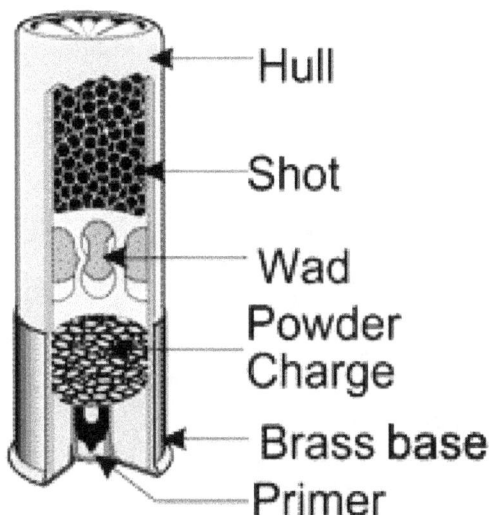

Hull

Shot

Wad

Powder
Charge

Brass base

Primer

Shot Type

The smaller the number the larger the shot:

Birdshot Selection	Lead/Tungsten	Steel
Quail, dove	71/2 - 8 shot	
Rabbit	6 - 71/2 shot	
Squirrel	6 shot	
Turkey, pheasant	4 - 6 shot	5 - 6 shot
Ducks, low	4 – 6 shot	2 – 4 shot
Ducks, high	2 – 4 shot	BB – 2 shot
Geese	BB - 2 shot	BBB - 1 shot

Understanding Ammunition

Buckshot

Buckshot is used for hunting larger game, such as deer. It is also used in police or tactical shotguns for defensive, police and military use. Buckshot is categorized by number with the smaller numbers being larger shot.

Size shot	Pellets/oz
000	6 pellets
00	8 pellets
0	9 pellets

48

Understanding Ammunition

1	10 pellets
2	15 pellets
3	18 pellets
4	21 pellets

Buckshot is largely responsible for the shotguns bad-to-the-bone image, particularly due to its stopping power. It has the ability to give you rifle like power at close quarters while minimizing over penetration or extended range. Another key benefit of buckshot is the pattern spread as it gives most people the ability to make quicker hits on moving targets vs. that associated with a single projectile, like a rifle or handgun bullet.

Understanding Ammunition

Slugs

Slugs allow your shotgun to become a short range or poor man's rifle.

Standard Slugs – is a huge hunk of lead, many may have grooves to induce some degree of rotation when fired through a smooth bore.

Saboted Slugs - contain a smaller projectile, which are typically wrapped in plastic in order to cause the diameter of the projectile to be the same as the bore. If you are planning to shoot saboted slugs you should have a rifled barrel. Saboted slugs can increase the effective range of your shotgun.

Understanding Ammunition

Penetration – Shotguns should be set up to allow sufficient penetration to handle the job. Over penetration should be avoided to reduce the ability of accidental injures (specialty set ups...00 buck, slugs, bird shot on ammo carriers).

When a shotgun is selected primarily for antipersonnel use, the choices of ammunition tend to decrease significantly and are typically limited to:

- Birdshot
- Buckshot or
- Slugs

Birdshot is rarely used for anything beyond home defense where engagement distances tend to be very close. Birdshot will often have sufficient stopping power for traditional home encounters or for historic pistol defense distances. Birdshot size 71/2 is typically a good choice. Care should be considered when selecting the hotter birdshot loads as the increased velocity may lead to increased/over penetration, which may not be required inside of 10 yards.

Most shotguns will pattern differently with different types of ammunition. Consequently, trial and error is necessary to find the optimal ammunition for your weapon and your desires. The most important selection in buckshot should be pattern reliability. While the best efficiency is obtained by keeping the shot charge together as far as possible thereby minimizing its shot spread, however shot spread is what gives you the greatest margin for error and allows you to make shots under tougher conditions than often possible with a rifle or handgun (single projectile bullet).

Understanding Ammunition

Benefits of Understanding the Spread or Pattern of your shotgun

- To increase the ability to hit moving targets.
- To minimize mis-hits/collateral damage when firing at close or long range.
- To maximize your ability to neutralize a threat.

To pattern your shotgun, you will need to go to the range bringing with you your shotgun, shotgun shells and some pieces of paper at least 40-inches square. To assist in centering the pattern as much as possible on the paper draw a black 2-inch dot in the center of the paper. Place the paper against an appropriate backstop and measure the precise distance you desire to evaluate.

Step up to the distance line, aim at the black dot and fire. After placing your weapon on safe, walk downrange and draw a circle around the pattern. To accurately evaluate your patterns, fire a minimum of three patterns of each load, shot size and choke at each distance of interest.

Distance	Pattern Size	Load	Manufacturer
7 yards			
10 yards			
15 yards			
20 yards			
25 yards			
50 yards			

Understanding Ammunition

Continue this process with multiple types of ammunition from multiple manufacturers until you find the optimal load and manufacturer type that best performs in your weapon.

If this shotgun is for home defense, it is highly recommended you become familiar with the farthest distance you may have to potentially engage an adversary in your home. Understanding the engagement distances in conjunction with your pattern associated with them, will enhance your effectiveness with the tool.

Understanding Ammunition

10 Yard Pattern Birdshot from Mossberg 590 Cylinder Bore Barrel

- Winchester Super-speed #8 Shot
- Pattern Spread L15" x W14"

Understanding Ammunition

10 Yard Pattern 00 Buckshot from Mossberg 590 Cylinder
Bore Barrel

- Hornady Tap #00 Buckshot Personal Defense Ammo
- Pattern Spread L 2.5 " x W 3.5 "

Understanding Ammunition

15 Yard Slug from Mossberg 590 Cylinder Bore Barrel

- Brenneke Black Magic Magnum 3" Slug
- Single Projectile ¾" hole

Understanding Ammunition

Maximizing your Shotguns Effectiveness – Engagement Zones

Green Light Zone – Typically within 7 yards, at this distance the shot pattern has not had any discernible ability to expand. If the target is hit at this distance the impact is usually pretty decisive. Heightened accuracy is typically associated with the operator's ability to index the muzzle or the sights on the target. A perfect sight picture at this distance is usually not required and tactically is probably not realistic if your adversary is armed. At this distance proximity can negate skill.

Understanding Ammunition

Yellow Light Zone – Typically 10 to 30 yards, at this distance the shot pattern has had the ability to expand and create a pretty defined spread, which may allow you to use that spread to enhance your ability to hit a moving target or give you more margin for error. This is the distance where the shotgun typically out-performs most handguns. The sights should be used to help enhance accuracy.

When dealing with moving targets, this is where the saying "you don't aim a shotgun you point one" applies. You allow the benefit of the pattern spread to aid you in hitting your target.

Understanding Ammunition

Red Light Zone – Historically beyond 35 yards (30 – 50 yards), is where the shotgun may start to lose a large degree of its effectiveness. You may increase the reach by switching to slugs, used a restrictive choke, or higher velocity ammunition. With shot vs. slugs this is where the adversary may have the ability to walk through the pattern because the pattern becomes so wide the pellets may go around the target or have reduced/limited impact. This is the distance where some shotguns may be rendered less effective.

Switching to slugs allows your shotgun to still be effective and become a short-range rifle; and with training may allow you to engage an adversary up to 100 yards. Sights are highly encouraged at this distance, particularly since you are firing a single projectile.

Understanding Ammunition

Cleaning your Shotgun

All new shotguns should be thoroughly inspected and cleaned before firing. When a shotgun is fired it accumulates dirt, gunpowder residue and other foreign particles which may make your firearm prone to malfunctions, corrosion or unnecessary wear if not properly maintained. Shotguns left unattended or stored for long periods of time may also become susceptible to dirt and dust which can also adversely impact operations.

Before cleaning, first make sure your firearm is unloaded! Now check it again to make sure it is unloaded! Remove all ammunition and store it securely in a separate room.

Understanding Ammunition

- Field Strip Pump Action or Semi-Automatic Shotguns (please refer to your owner's manual).
- Clean regularly with some type of solvent (Gunslick, Break Free, Hoppes etc), cotton patches, bore snakes, nylon or wire brushes, jags, bore rods.
- Lubricate with a light gun oil after cleaning (check your owner's manual for the recommended type)
- Wipe down the outside of your firearm with a gun friendly cloth suitable for your type of firearm (Kleen-Bore Silicone Gun Reel Cloth).
- If storing please store your shotgun empty and out of the reach of unintended users (all firearms should be stored unloaded, with trigger locks and then stored in a locked container or safe whenever possible).

Keep your shotgun clean and lubricated. This is a major tool to assist you in protecting your family, client or other team members. Your job should be to help minimize the potential for weapon malfunctions caused by a dirty or poorly conditioned or maintained weapon.

Understanding Ammunition

Chapter 4

Shotgun Marksmanship Fundamentals

Yes that is a 20 round drum. This is not your father's semi-automatic shotgun!

Shotgun Marksmanship Fundamentals

Shotgun Marksmanship Fundamentals

Like all good repeatable skills good shotgun performance is built on a stable platform of strong fundamentals. Below are the keys to consistent performance:

1. Grip
2. Stance
3. The Mount
4. Sight Alignment
5. Breath Control
6. Trigger Squeeze

The Grip

People often underestimate the importance of grip. Your grip is the primary thing that keeps you "one" with your weapon!

Shotgun Marksmanship Fundamentals

- With a shotgun your grip is largely influenced by the shotguns length of pull (the distance from the butt to the center of the trigger).
- Your grip should be firm not tight.
- The pistol grip or stock is grasped firmly with the strong hand, and the forefinger is placed on the side of the receiver with the thumb and remaining fingers wrapped around the pistol grip or stock. Firm rearward pressure should be exerted to help keep the shotgun butt firmly in the shoulder, reducing the effects of recoil.
- Once your sights are on the target, the trigger finger will go into the trigger guard, placed naturally on the trigger and care should be taken to ensure the trigger finger can move independently without dragging on the side of the receiver. A proper grip allows the trigger to be moved straight to the rear without disturbing sight alignment.
- New shooters often invoke tension into their shooting by gripping the weapon too tightly in an effort to attempt to reduce or manage recoil.
- Your support hand should rest comfortably on the forearm of your shotgun.
- Vertical grips or posts will often assist in helping manage recoil.

Shotgun Marksmanship Fundamentals

Stance

There are multiple shooting and/or carry positions that the shooter should learn to operate from in order to enhance their effectiveness and their versatility when deploying their shotgun.

.

Shotgun Marksmanship Fundamentals

- Your stance must be steady and comfortable so that you don't become fatigued too easily.
- Your weight is slightly forward. This helps reduce felt recoil. Weight favors the front leg vs. rear.
- Your strong side (the side the gun is mounted on) leg is slightly back. This helps you maintain balance.
- Standing bladed or square may be a matter of choice or tactical necessity.
- Standing bladed to the threat slightly narrows your body, making you a smaller target. However, for those providing protective services or wearing body armor, standing more squared to the target provides additional body mass to cover your client. It also reduces exposure to your armpit the weakest part of your bullet proof vest.
- Knees should be slightly bent to help provide natural shock absorption.
- If shooting a target on the move your stance will typically be slightly open.

Shotgun Marksmanship Fundamentals

Enhancing your Weapon Mount

Shotgun Marksmanship Fundamentals

What you will need:

Outside Practice – live range
One Target, Target Stand and a Marker.

Set your target up to a height 6 feet tall. Place a 50 cent piece size mark on the target center mass approximately at the nipple line.

Inside Practice – non range
Check and make sure the rifle is unloaded.
Remove all ammunition from the room.
Large Mirror, Masking Tape or One Target, Target Stand and a Marker.

Set your target up to a height 6 feet tall. Place a 50 cent piece size mark on the target center mass. If you are practicing inside with a mirror, place an X on the mirror center mass approximately at the nipple line.

Shotgun Marksmanship Fundamentals

Your start position should look something like the pictures above on the left. From the low ready position, (without a timer or stop watch) raise the muzzle and mount your shotgun; placing your sights on the intended point of aim.

Drill 1

Do 20 reps of your mount at 1/4 speed – this is designed to familiarize and engrain the basic mechanics for this drill. Each repetition of the mount should be conducted on a mental count, while maintaining fluidity of motion. It should sound something like this – "1 Bring the Weapon Up, 2 Break the Round, 3 Call the sight placement/this should have been the last sight picture you saw after you pulled the trigger (if you are on the live fire range – you should be able to call the shot placement/point of impact"). This will aid in follow through which is one of the keys to accuracy.

Shotgun Marksmanship Fundamentals

Do 20 reps at 1/4 speed

Drill 2

Do 20 reps 1/4 speed (with your eyes closed)

Again, this drill is designed to further engrain the mechanics for this drill, and help you create your natural body indexing position. Each repetition of the mount should be conducted on a mental count, while maintaining fluidity of motion. It should sound something like this – 1Bring the Shotgun Up, 2 Break the Round, 3 Pause and open your eyes and see where your sights are aligned in relation to your desired point of impact. This will aid in follow through which is one of the keys to accuracy. You are looking for consistency and fluidity of motion. This is not a speed drill this is a fluidity of motion drill, designed to further remove the kinks.

Drill 3

Do 20 reps 1/2 speed (eyes open)

Repeat Drill 1 but at 1/2 speed. Again, you're looking for consistency and fluidity of motion. This is not a speed drill. This is a fluidity of motion drill, designed to remove the kinks.

Drill 4

Do 20 reps at Full speed (eyes open)

At this time your mount should feel considerably faster but not rushed. "Full speed" should be as fast as you can get

Shotgun Marksmanship Fundamentals

the weapon up from low ready onto the target while maintaining control over your body mechanics and a fluid motion on the mount. If you start to jerk the pattern off target, cut back on the speed until you can maintain the fluidity of motion. A fast mount time for this is drill is in the 1.25 second range. The purpose of this drill is to build the consistency and economy of motion speed will come. Your goal is to eliminate over-travel (moving the sights past your intended point of aim).

Consistency + Economy of Motion = Speed

Since the first gunfight shooters have had an ongoing quest for speed. Particularly when it comes to engaging multiple adversaries or in close quarter encounters. You often don't need to learn to shoot faster; you often just need to shoot sooner. With ongoing practice you will start to become more consistent with mounting your tactical rifle. As you enhance the mechanics of your mount you will start to bring your weapon into your sightline sooner, giving you the ability to break the round earlier which will by default make your shots quicker!

Shotgun Marksmanship Fundamentals

Eye Dominance

Like most dynamic activities, shooting requires good hand eye coordination. Before we can effectively work on sight alignment we must first establish if we are right or left eye dominant. Below is an exercise to help you determine your eye dominance.

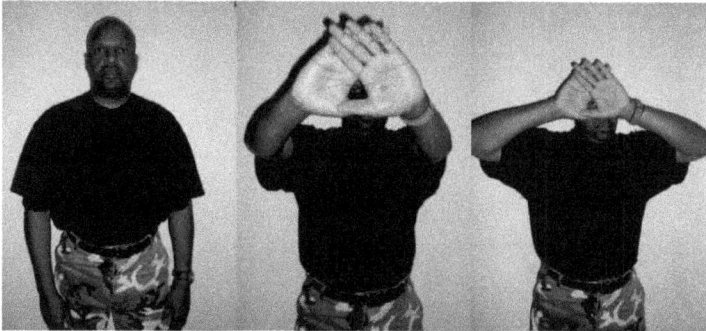

1. While standing with your hands at your side, focus on an object out in the distance.
2. Now extend your hands straight out in front of you; one hand over the other (and touching) making a small quarter size hole in between your hands still focusing on the object at a distance.
3. Now bring your hands back toward your face, continuing to look at the object until they are only a few inches away from you face. The hole between your hands will be in front of your dominant eye (if you make a decision to shoot one eye closed, make sure the eye you keep open is your dominant eye and you work to align everything else in relation to your dominant eye).

Shotgun Marksmanship Fundamentals

Sight Alignment

Shotgun Marksmanship Fundamentals

What is the difference between sight picture and sight alignment?

- Sight alignment refers to the relationship between the front sight and rear sight (dominant eye if there is no rear sight).
- Sight picture is what you see superimposed on the other end of your front sight (the superimposed image should be slightly out of focus with the clearer focus on the front sight).

Sights on most shotguns may consist of a front bead, blade front post or red dot optic.

- It is important to understand that sight alignment with a shotgun is often obtained through proper gun mount.
- Sights on shotguns are used to verify alignment, not establish it.
- In shots less than 25 yards perfect sight alignment and sight picture is not as critical.
- If the front sight is on the target your point of impact will generally be fairly close to your point of aim.
- In close quarter you generally will rely on just a flash sight picture before breaking the shot.
- In close quarter instinctive or point shooting, many shots are taken based on muscle memory, or indexing off of body parts, the muzzle with minimal focus on the front sights.
- For long range shots or typically shots employing slugs; the rear sights or ghost rings are typically utilized to enhance accuracy.

Shotgun Marksmanship Fundamentals

Moving Targets

Once you learn how to mount a shotgun properly there are only four ways to miss a target:

- Above
- Below
- Behind
- In front

Once you learn how to swing the gun on a horizontal plane, on the same line as the target, or portion of the target you wish to hit, then the only thing we have to do is now work on lead or trail. If the target is moving faster than we are, we rely on leading the target and the shot pattern (the target will move into the pattern) to hit the target. If the target is moving slower than we, are we rely on trailing the target and shot pattern (the pattern will catch up to the target) to hit the target. Finding a local skeet range and renting a skeet shotgun will significantly enhance your ability to understand lead and perform better in tactical movement situations.

Shotgun Marksmanship Fundamentals

Reactive or Point Shooting

Reactive shooting like all close quarter engagements involves quick reactions and involves good hand eye coordination. In reactive or point shooting our focus is primarily on the adversary. Learning to watch your adversary or staying alert while searching for your adversary is of critical importance. The effective introduction of your weapon will come as a conditioned response with proper training.

Once you learn to mount your shotgun consistently, your front sight will become like a third eye, and your subconscious will learn to move the weapon to the threat. When scanning the target be highly conscious of focusing on the adversary hands prior to scanning the remainder of the body.

Shotgun Marksmanship Fundamentals

Breathing

- Breathing control is much less important in shotgun shooting than in rifle or handgun shooting, as we typically point a shotgun versus aiming it unless shooting a slug (relying on the pattern to neutralize the threat versus the precision of a single projectile).
- It is still important enough to cause a miss, especially at long range (25 yards or more).
- Breathing causes movement of the chest and a corresponding movement in the shotgun and its sights. To minimize this movement and the effect it has on your aim, learn to control your breathing and extend your natural respiratory pause for a few seconds during the final aiming and firing process. In a dynamic and/or close quarter encounter this will be extremely challenging.
- When firing rapid fire shots, it may be necessary to take small "baby breaths" to produce a respiratory pause between each shot. The respiratory pauses help you maintain your natural point of aim; however, holding your breath too long may lessen your ability to maintain focus on the sights.
- Relaxation prevents undue muscle strain and reduces excessive movement. If proper relaxation is achieved, your natural point of aim and sight alignment is more easily maintained.

Shotgun Marksmanship Fundamentals

Trigger Squeeze

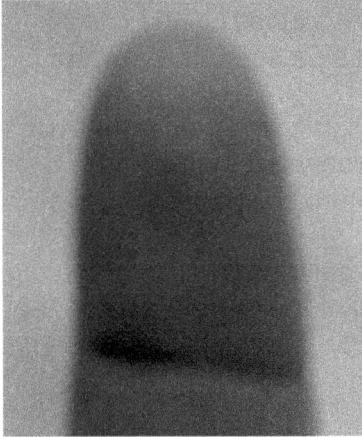

Trigger Squeeze basics

- The key to trigger control is a steady rearward squeeze of the trigger (you often hear people refer to it as pressing the trigger, I have never pressed a trigger in my life, although I have pulled many of them…remember pull does not mean jerk).
- The trigger finger should slip into the trigger guard from its "safety" position on the frame only when you are ready to shoot (otherwise it stays on the trigger guard along the side of the frame).
- Guard against "slapping" the trigger, once you make contact with the trigger.
- (A). Once inside of the trigger guard, the area of the first pad of the forefinger between the center of the pad and first knuckle should touch the trigger (try to shoot off the center of your index fingers fingerprint). (B). Having the trigger touched down in the crevice

Shotgun Marksmanship Fundamentals

of the first joint of the finger will cause the gun to pull
to the left or right and slightly down instead of staying
exactly where the sights are aligned.

- The trigger squeeze should be a smooth rearward
  steady motion.
- Watch the front sight and align it with the target while
  the trigger is being pulled rearward (not jerked).
  When the trigger breaks should come as a surprise
  to you.
- You should be able to call your shots by remembering
  where the front sight or top of the muzzle was on the
  target, the moment the trigger broke.

Shotgun Marksmanship Fundamentals

Trigger Practice

- Practice Trigger control by dry-firing your shotgun at home.
- Use a target on the wall.
- Make sure the shotgun is unloaded (check at least three times, after you have put all ammunition in another room)!
- Using snap caps or dummy practice rounds will allow you to perform the other weapons handling skills in conjunction with your trigger practice.
- Then, practice all the earlier points while aiming at your "target."
- Never dry-fire more than 50 times in each session, before taking a break.
- When you feel fatigued take a break to allow you to maintain your concentration and technique (during your break re-read all of your instructions to allow you to correct any mistakes from the earlier session).
- You cannot dry-fire too much!
- Focusing on the front sight and trigger control are the keys to shooting well.

Stopping Power & Shot Placement

When it comes to stopping a threat you stop it one of two ways, either psychologically or physiologically. That is why I like long guns when it comes to personal defense whenever possible. Shotguns are nasty, they rip flesh and bone (particularly with 00 Buck). For a short distance shotgun bullets move faster than many handgun bullets and deliver more energy. When you shoot something with slug, you aren't just making a hole, but you are making a massive hole

Shotgun Marksmanship Fundamentals

and causing severe trauma in the tissue surrounding the hole.

When you say psychologically, that means the adversary quits because their mind says "hold on, not only does he have a gun, he has a big gun!" That is a huge hole I am facing. Think about the intimidating factor of when you see the wrong end of the muzzle below:

Physiologically their body says "hold on that hurts and I don't want any more", or you hit them with a fatal wound and they

Shotgun Marksmanship Fundamentals

fall to the floor. It is important that readers understand the two leading theories on Stopping Power and Shot Placement if they are looking to rely on a Physiological stop.

- Stopping Power – is the ability (or lack thereof) of a particular type of ammunition to incapacitate an adversary.
- There are three major considerations:
  1. Do I need flexibility in the pattern (greater spread)?
  2. Do I need a restrictive pattern (reduced spread or single projectile)?
  3. Do I need the shot or projectile to travel over a longer distance?
- There is no exact science when it comes to selection...the best you can do is make an informed, intelligent decision about gauge type and shot preference and situation application.

If you feel deadly force is your only option then you should understand these basics. The shot or slug incapacitates its target in two ways:

1. One way is by causing enough blood loss in the adversary to stop him (sometimes referred to as draining the pump).

2. The second way is damaging the central nervous system (brain or spine). A brain shot is pretty conclusive, the challenge is a clean brain shot is difficult for most people to execute, particularly in a stressful situation (sometimes referred to as turning off the power), with a restricted shot pattern or single projectile (slug).

Shotgun Marksmanship Fundamentals

The target zones below will generally address the concern:

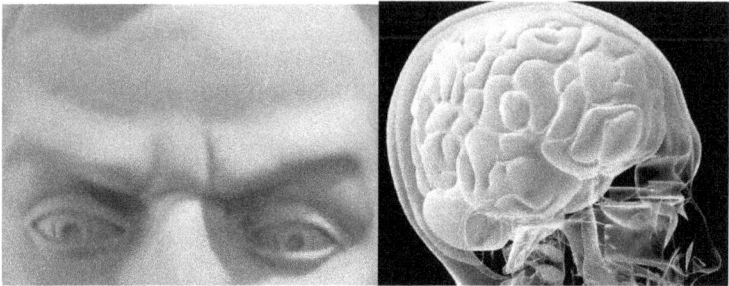

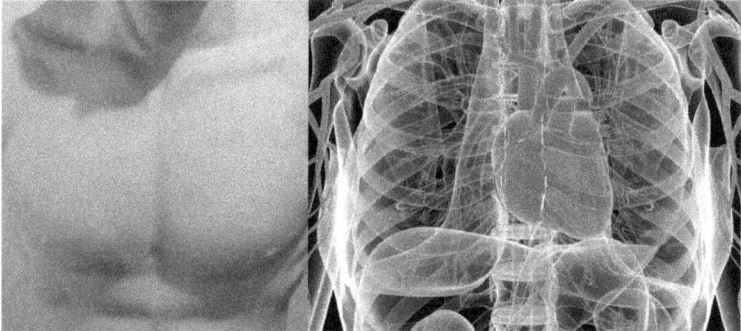

Chapter 5

Carry Positions

"Without knowledge, skill cannot be focused. Without skill, strength cannot be brought to bear and without strength, knowledge may not be applied."
Alexander the Great's Chief Physician

Carry Positions

African Carry

Carry Positions

- This is primarily a low-threat carry method.
- Shotgun is slung over the support side shoulder with the sling side facing forward.
- The muzzle may be pointed up or down, pointing the muzzle down aids in concealment or when there is limited clearance.
- Safety on or off is a matter of preference, duty requirements or your level of safety consciousness.
- To react to a threat, simply grab the forearm of the shotgun with the support hand. The muzzle is then raised toward the perceived threat, while rotating the shotgun up bringing the sights to the top, and pulling the shotgun back into the shoulder pocket, and aligning the cheek onto the comb/buttstock.

Carry Positions

American Carry

Carry Positions

- This is primarily a low-threat carry method.
- Shotgun is slung over the strong side shoulder with the sling side facing forward.
- The muzzle is pointed up.
- Safety on or off is a matter of preference, duty requirements or your level of safety consciousness.
- To react to a threat simply push the sling forward with the strong hand, with the reaction hand reach under the strong side arm and grab the forearm of the shotgun with the reaction hand push the muzzle forward toward the adversary, as you pull the strong side arm out of the sling, reacquire the pistol grip pulling the shotgun back into the shoulder pocket, and aligning the cheek onto the comb/buttstock.

Carry Positions

Tactical Carry

Carry Positions

- This is primarily a low to moderate-threat carry method.
- Is executed with a tactical sling to help reduce fatigue from carrying the weapon over an extended period of time.
- One or both hands are placed on the weapon depending on the threat level.
- The strong side hand is held above waist high on the shotgun wrist.
- The support side hand may be held on the forearm or hang free in order to perform other functions depending on the threat level.
- The muzzle is indexed downward.
- Your trigger finger is indexed along side of the trigger guard.
- Safety on or off is a matter of preference, duty requirements or your level of safety consciousness.
- To react to a threat simply move the muzzle toward the perceived threat.

Carry Positions

Rhodesian Carry

Carry Positions

- This is primarily a low-threat carry method.
- Both hands are placed on the weapon.
- The strong side hand is held slightly above waist high.
- The support side hand is held slightly below waist high and is relaxed (this allows the muzzle to be indexed slightly downward).
- Your trigger finger is indexed along side of the trigger guard.
- Safety on or off is a matter of preference, duty requirements or your level of safety consciousness.
- To react to a threat simply move the muzzle toward the perceived threat.

Carry Positions

Underarm Assault Position

Carry Positions

- This is a moderate to high-threat carry method.
- The buttstock is placed high under the armpit against the pectoral muscle.
- The butt is placed just inside of the armpit.
- Both hands are placed on the weapon and are held approximately chest high, your elbows are angled down toward the ground.
- Your trigger finger is indexed along side of the trigger guard.
- Safety on or off is a matter of preference, duty requirements or your level of safety consciousness.
- You must learn to keep your dominant eye placed over the shotgun's barrel.
- Reacting to a threat or adversary is done by indexing your body on the target.
- This engagement is done with little to no sight picture (this position is typically used for shots within 7 yards).

Carry Positions

High-Ready (Hunter's Position)

Carry Positions

- This is a high-threat carry method.
- The buttstock is held slightly above the waist on the strong side.
- The butt is placed inside the strong side forearm.
- The support hand is held on the forearm with the elbow angled down toward the ground.
- The muzzle is angled upward, but below eye level to allow the shooter to see over the muzzle.
- Your trigger finger is indexed along side of the trigger guard.
- Safety on or off is a matter of preference, duty requirements or your level of safety consciousness.
- Reacting to a threat or adversary is done by quickly moving the weapon down and indexing the sights on the target.
- The butt of the shotgun is then pulled back into the shoulder pocket as you prepare to break the round.
- This position is often used to search outdoors, and it is not recommended for:
  -indoors or close quarter searches as it may bring your muzzle to close to your adversary.
  -dealing with potential threats that are anticipated to come from a lower position as it may take too much time to bring the muzzle down to the threat and the muzzle may inadvertently impact your ability for fast acquisition to the lower threat position.

Carry Positions

Low-Ready (Search)

Carry Positions

- This is a high-threat carry method.
- The buttstock is already placed in the shoulder pocket.
- The support hand is held on the forearm with the elbow angled down toward the ground.
- The muzzle is angled downward, slightly below the waist.
- Your trigger finger is indexed along side of the trigger guard.
- Safety on or off is a matter of preference, duty requirements or your level of safety consciousness.
- Reacting to a threat or adversary is done by quickly moving the muzzle up and indexing the sights on the target.
- This position is often used for searches, close quarter and fast movement scenarios.

Carry Positions

Indoor Low-Ready (Extreme Close Quarter - Indoor Search)

Carry Positions

- This is a high-threat carry method.
- The buttstock is already placed in the shoulder pocket.
- The support hand is held on the forearm in close proximity to your support side leg with the elbow pointed behind you.
- The muzzle is angled downward and angled anywhere from 12 to 18 inches in front of and slightly outside of your lead foot (be careful not to cover your foot with the muzzle).
- Your trigger finger is indexed along side of the trigger guard.
- Safety on or off is a matter of preference, duty requirements or your level of safety consciousness.
- Reacting to a threat or adversary is done by moving the muzzle up and indexing the sights on the target.
- This position is often used for indoor searches, and extreme close quarter environments.
- For extreme close quarter searches:
  -employing a modified underarm position where the strong side hand may be placed alongside slightly above the ribcage and underarm, the buttstock exposed through and behind the armpit.
  -employing a tactical sling to carry the shotgun and transitioning to a handgun may be a more efficient option.

Carry Positions

Supine

If you are in this position it has probably come as the result of an "oh shit" moment.   It may be the result of a trip and fall; you may have been knocked to the ground by your adversary, or from being blast into this position.

Carry Positions

- Legs, knees and feet are wide apart.
- Feet are angled out.
- Weapon is forward on the torso not mounted on the shoulder, you will need to drive the weapon forward to find the holographic dot or your fixed sights.
- For CQB you may be relying on indexing off the top of the muzzle as opposed to utilizing the sights at all taking advantage of the pattern spread.
- This allows you to get a quicker sight picture while maintaining a lower profile.
- Keep your legs spread wide to avoid an intersection with your line of fire. Keep your feet angled out as you engage the threat and discharge your weapon.
- Try to get off of your back as soon as tactically possible.
- Remember to search and assess from each position as you go from Supine to Kneeling to Standing or whatever is your desired platform.

Chapter 6
Shotgun Reloading

You don't want to be a visitor in a gunfight!

Shotgun Reloading

Maintaining Continuity of Fire

If you are not shooting because you are out of ammunition, then you have been reduced to being a visitor in a gunfight. Not fun. Learning how to efficiently reload your shotgun can literally be the difference between life and death.

There are three primary types of reloading:

- Administrative Reload
- Tactical Reload
- Emergency Reload

Shotgun Reloading

Administrative Reload

Administrative Reload – is a proactive and preparatory loading procedure and is done in advance of a fire-fight or engagement.   It is done under a no stress environment.

Shotgun Reloading

- Hold the shotgun in the strong hand.
- Keep your finger off the trigger and the muzzle pointed in a safe direction.
- Pull the forearm back thus opening the bolt (pump action) or pull the action lever back (semi-automatic shotguns).
- Retrieve a shell from your side-mounted or butt-mounted ammo carrier, belt-mounted ammo carrier or pocket with your support hand (allow the shell to ride low in your fingers, above the palm and in between your pinky and forefinger.
- Bring the support hand under the receiver and against the open ejection port and drop the shell into the ejection port.

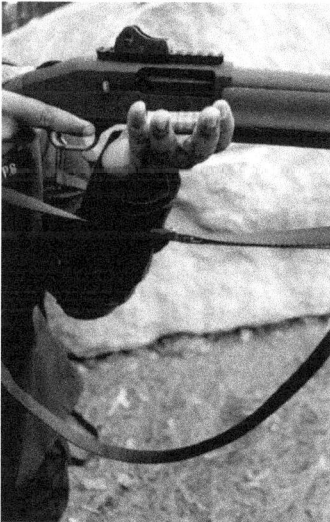

Shotgun Reloading

- Now using the empty support hand, close the action by either bringing the forearm forward or activating the slide action release button with your support hand for a semi-automatic weapon.

Loading the tubular magazine

- Hold the shotgun in the strong hand.
- Retrieve a shell or slug from your ammunition source (side-mounted, butt-mounted, belt-mounted or pocket).
- Bring the shell under the receiver and at a point just forward of the trigger guard loading port.
- Insert the shell forward into the tubular magazine, pushing it forward with your thumb.
- Continue to repeat the process until you have loaded your desired number of rounds.

Shotgun Reloading

Defensive or Tactical Storage Mode - involves loading the magazine, but keeping the chamber empty and the action closed. This allows you the ability to bring the shotgun into action quickly (by pumping the shotgun or activating the action lever) while incorporating an enhanced degree of safety.

Choosing to utilize the safety or not is a matter of personal preference, or duty requirements but consistency in either approach is encouraged to help develop muscle memory which will be of significant importance in a fire–fight. If the shotgun is being used for home defense care must be taken to ensure unwanted persons don't handle your loaded weapon.

Shotgun Reloading

Tactical Reload

Tactical Reload – is a proactive loading procedure which allows the operator to bring their gun back to desired capacity during the calm in the storm. This may be as the result of the bad guy is down or you have moved to cover during your actual fire-fight and desire to bring your weapon to full capacity in order to continue to handle your business

Shotgun Reloading

and maintain continuity of fire. Tactical reloading subscribes to the old adage of reload when you want to, not when you have to!

- Hold the shotgun in the strong hand.
- Keep your finger off the trigger and the muzzle pointed in a safe direction or in the direction of the adversary.
- Try to avoid executing a tactical reload while in the kill zone. Move to cover!
- Retrieve a shell or slug from your ammunition source (side-mounted, butt-mounted, belt-mounted, wrist or pocket).
- Bring the shell under the receiver and at a point just forward of the trigger guard loading port.
- Insert the shell forward into the tubular magazine, pushing it forward with your thumb.
- Continue to repeat the process until you have loaded your desired number of rounds.

Shotgun Reloading

Emergency Reload from the Bottom

Emergency Reload – is a reactive loading procedure and is done in the middle of a fire-fight or engagement.   It is done under a high-stress environment. It typically comes as the result of a click versus a bang with a pump shotgun or with a semi-auto shotgun the action locks open.

Shotgun Reloading

- If you have a back up weapon, it may be quicker to transition to a back up gun (pistol or other firearm) if not follow the below instructions.
- Hold the shotgun in the strong hand.
- Keep your finger off the trigger. However the muzzle should be pointed toward the adversary.
- Pull the forearm back thus opening the bolt (pump action) or pull the action lever back (semi-automatic shotguns).
- Retrieve a shell from your side action or butt mounted ammo carrier, belt mounted ammo carrier or pocket with your support hand (allow the shell to ride low in your fingers, above the palm and in between your pinky and forefinger.
- Bring the support hand under the receiver and against the open ejection port and drop the shell into the ejection port.
- Now using the empty support hand, close the action by either bringing the forearm forward or activating the slide action release button.
- Get back into the fight or move to cover.

Shotgun Reloading

Loading the Tubular Magazine

- Hold the shotgun in the strong hand.
- Retrieve a shell or slug from your ammunition source (side-mounted, butt-mounted, belt-mounted or pocket).
- Bring the shell under the receiver and at a point just forward of the trigger guard loading port.

Shotgun Reloading

- Insert the shell forward into the tubular magazine, pushing it forward with your thumb.
- Continue to repeat the process until you have loaded your desired number of rounds.

Other Reloading Options

Reloading from the Top

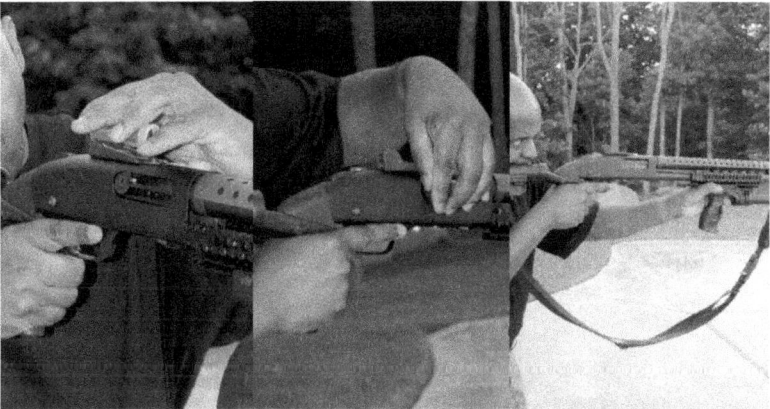

Administrative Reload – is a proactive and preparatory loading procedure and is done in advance of a fire-fight or engagement. It is done under a no stress environment.

- Hold the shotgun in the strong hand.
- Keep your finger off the trigger and the muzzle pointed in a safe direction.
- Pull the forearm back thus opening the bolt (pump action) or pull the action lever back (semi-automatic shotguns).

Shotgun Reloading

- Retrieve a shell from your side-mounted or butt-mounted ammo carrier, belt-mounted ammo carrier or pocket with your support hand (allow the shell to ride low in your fingers, below the palm and in between your pinky and forefinger.
- Bring the reaction/support hand over the receiver and against the open ejection port and drop the shell into the ejection port.
- Now using the empty reaction/support hand, close the action by either bringing the forearm forward or activating the slide action release button with your support hand for a semi-automatic weapon.
- The advantage of this procedure is the first shell is positioned closer to the chamber, this quicker to load.
- The disadvantage of this procedure is that if you are not careful you may drop the shell or slug as your hand is in a reverse cupped position.

Shotgun Reloading

- Load the remaining rounds under the receiver and at a point just forward of the trigger guard loading port (as described earlier). Insert the shell forward into the tubular magazine, pushing it forward with the strong side your thumb. Continue to repeat the process until you have loaded your desired number of rounds.

Shotgun Reloading

Emergency Reloading from the Top

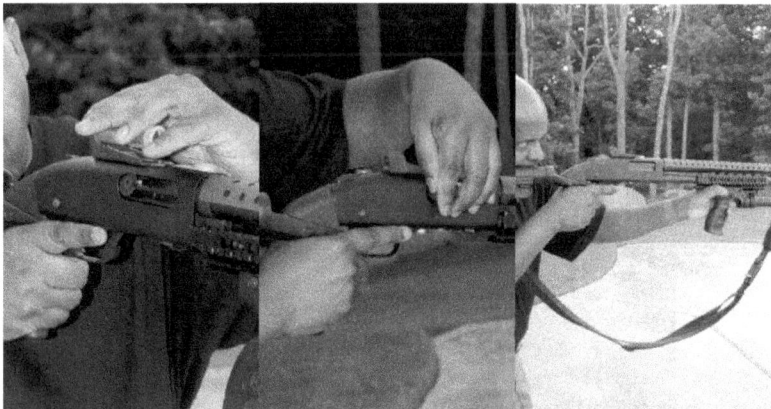

Emergency Reload – is a reactive loading procedure and is done in the middle of a fire-fight or engagement.   It is done under a high-stress environment. It typically comes as the result of a click versus a bang with a pump shotgun or with a semi-auto shotgun the action locks open.

- If you have a back up weapon, it may be quicker to transition to a back up gun (pistol or other firearm) if not follow the below instructions.
- Try to move to over or at a minimum try to create distance.
- Hold the shotgun in the strong hand.
- Pull the forearm back thus opening the bolt (pump action) or pull the action lever back (semi-automatic shotguns).
- Retrieve a shell from your side-mounted or butt-mounted ammo carrier, belt-mounted ammo carrier or pocket with your support hand (allow the shell to ride

Shotgun Reloading

low in your fingers, below the palm and between your pinky and forefinger.

- Bring the reaction/support hand over the receiver and against the open ejection port, dropping the shell into the ejection port.
- Now using the empty reaction/support hand, close the action by either bringing the forearm forward or activating the slide action release button with your support hand for a semi-automatic weapon.
- The advantage of this procedure is speed. By coming over the top, the shell is positioned closer to the chamber. Therefore it is quicker to load the initial shell or slug.
- The disadvantage of this procedure is that if you are not careful you may drop the shell or slug as your hand is in a reverse cupped position.
- Load the remaining rounds under the receiver and at a point just forward of the trigger guard loading port (as described earlier). Insert the shell forward into the tubular magazine, pushing it forward with the strong side thumb. Continue to repeat the process until you have loaded your desired number of rounds.

Shotgun Reloading

Side Saddle Reload/Forearm Reload

Shotgun Reloading

Side Saddle or Forearm Reload is an alternate Tactical Reload (proactive) loading procedure which allows the operator to bring their gun back to desired capacity during the calm in the storm. This may be as the result of the bad guy is down or you have moved to cover during your actual fire-fight and desire to bring your weapon to full capacity in order to continue to handle your business and maintain continuity of fire.

- Hold the shotgun in your reaction/support hand and rotate the shotgun outward resting it on your reaction/support hand forearm.
- The butt of the shotgun is either into your reaction/support side hip or under your strong side armpit for enhanced stability.
- Keep your finger off the trigger and the muzzle pointed in a safe direction or in the direction of the adversary.
- Try to avoid executing a tactical reload while in the kill zone (move to cover).
- Retrieve a shell or slug from your side saddle with your strong hand and insert it under the receiver and at a point just forward of the trigger guard loading port.
- Insert the shell forward into the tubular magazine, pushing it forward with the strong side thumb.
- Continue to repeat the process until you have loaded your desired number of rounds.

Shotgun Reloading

- Then with your reaction/support side hand grabbing the forearm and your strong side grabbing the wrist of the shotgun rotate the shotgun back into the mount position and continue to handle your business.
- This technique is good for the shooter who may not have the strength to keep the shotgun held on fire control (shoulder level pointed toward adversary or potential threat area).

Shotgun Reloading

Wrist Reload

Shotgun Reloading

Wrist Reload Explained

The Wrist Reload is another Tactical Reload (proactive) loading procedure which allows the operator to bring their gun back to desired capacity during the calm in the storm. Again, this may be as the result of the bad guy being down or you have moved to cover during your actual fire-fight and desire to bring your weapon to full capacity in order to continue to handle your business and maintain continuity of fire.

- Hold the shotgun in your reaction/support hand and rotate the shotgun outward resting it on your reaction/support hand forearm.
- The butt of the shotgun is either into your reaction/support side hip or under your strong side armpit for enhanced stability.

Hip Supported   Underarm Supported

Shotgun Reloading

- Keep your finger off the trigger and the muzzle pointed in a safe direction or in the direction of the adversary.
- Try to avoid executing a tactical reload while in the kill zone (move to cover).
- Retrieve a shell or slug from your wrist mounted ammo carrier (it should be in a similar position to where you would execute the side saddle reload) with your strong hand and insert it under the receiver and at a point just forward of the trigger guard loading port.
- Insert the shell forward into the tubular magazine, pushing it forward with the strong side thumb (upper right photo prior page).
- Continue to repeat the process until you have loaded your desired number of rounds.
- Then with your reaction/support side hand grabbing the forearm and your strong side grabbing the wrist of the shotgun, rotate the shotgun back into the mount position and continue to handle your business (lower left and right photos prior page).

Shotgun Reloading

Transitioning to your Secondary and Reloading the Shotgun

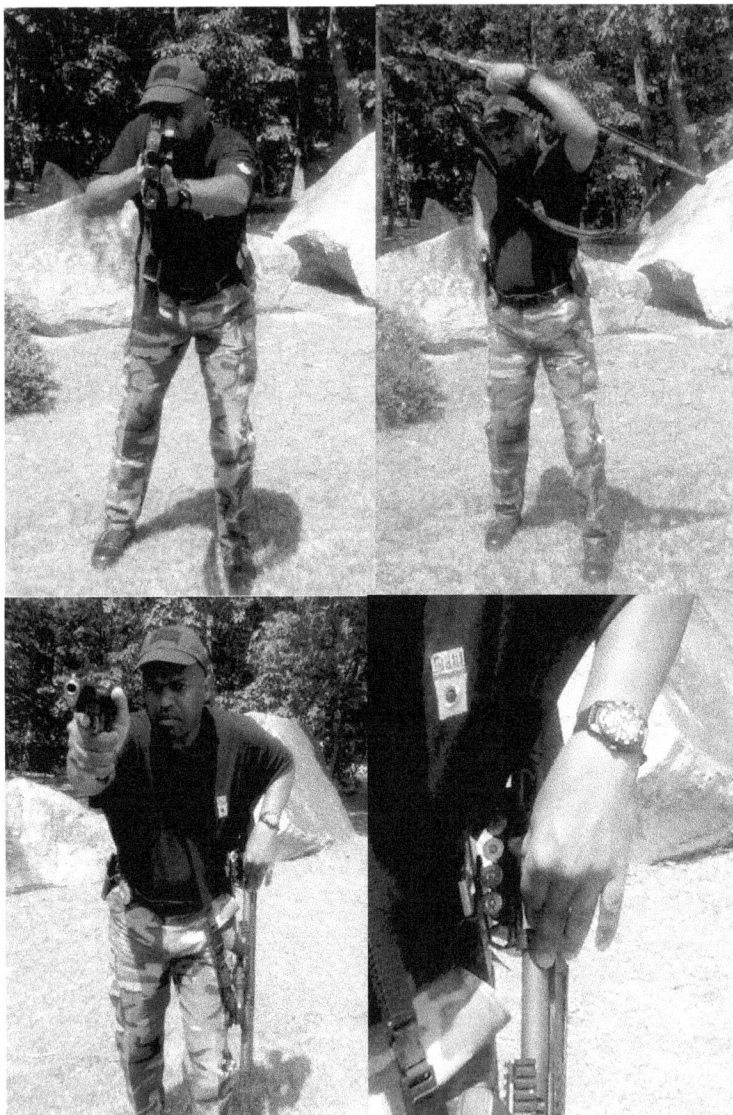

Shotgun Reloading

Transitioning to the Secondary Explained

- As a result of your shotgun going click and not bang, your reaction side hand in the photos on the previous page grabs the wrist of the shotgun raising it over year head, as you simultaneously grab your handgun with your weapon side hand.
- As you either continue engaging the threat or cover the threat if it has been neutralized. Use your reaction side hand to continue to load the tubular magazine of the shotgun bringing it back to your desired capacity.
- Once you have loaded the shotgun to its desired capacity, reach down and grab the forearm of the shotgun. As you raise the muzzle back onto the threat rotate the shotgun forearm toward 9:00 rotating the sights up pulling the shotgun back into the mount position as you simultaneously holster your handgun.
- Continue to cover the threat as required.

Shotgun Reloading

Emergency Reloading the Saiga

Shotgun Reloading

Emergency Reloading the Saiga Explained

- At this point the weapon goes click and not bang. Depending on your training and muscle memory you may have tugged on the magazine to make sure it was seated prior to attempting to rack the bolt to chamber a new round.
- Remember the slide does not lock back on an empty magazine with the Saiga 12.
- Grab a replacement magazine from your ammo carrier, tactical vest or pocket (upper left photo prior page).
- Use the back of your replacement magazine to activate your magazine release lever (upper right photo prior page).
- Now insert your replacement magazine into the magazine well and tug it to make sure it is seated (lower left photo prior page).
- Reach under and around to the bolt action lever. This may be done with the reaction hand thumb (I prefer the thumb as it helps me guarantee may hand doesn't slip) or the outside-bottom side of the palm (knife hand) and activate the bolt action release lever (lower right photo prior page).

Shotgun Reloading

Reloading Guiding Principles

- The major rule of thumb around reloading is "reload when you want to, not when you have to!"
- A gun fight is nothing more than a fight that involves a gun. If you were having a fist fight with an adversary you would typically hit your adversary as hard as you can as often as you can, until they are no longer a threat. A gun fight is no different.
- There is only one reason to reload, to give you the ability to continue to fire.
- To truly maintain continuity of fire requires you to leave one round in the chamber and discarding the empty or partial magazine in order to replace it with a fresh magazine or in tubular magazines to keep filling the magazine to its desired capacity.
- Keeping one round in the chamber allows you the ability to take a shot real-time during the reload if required, and eliminates the need to operate the slide release.

Shotgun Reloading

Transitioning to Alternate Ammunition

Transitioning to alternate ammunition may be required in the middle of a fire-fight or in advance of a potential encounter. Before transitioning you must consider is it tactically realistic or desirable to stop engaging the adversary at this time, in order to change ammunition?

Often transitioning to alternate ammunition is associated with shifting from Buckshot to Slugs. Below are some possible considerations when transition to a slug is often considered:

- When the target has moved outside of effective zone of the buckshot or other type of shot load.
- When a more precise shot is required via a single projectile (i.e. hostage type of situation).
- When increased penetration is required (i.e. punching through potential cover of an adversary, firing into an engine block etc.).

However transitioning from Slugs or Buckshot to Birdshot or some other type of lighter load may be desirable if over-penetration concerns are of importance; or if the need to have greater pattern spread (often required to hit a moving target) is required.

Shotgun Reloading

Transition the Ammunition

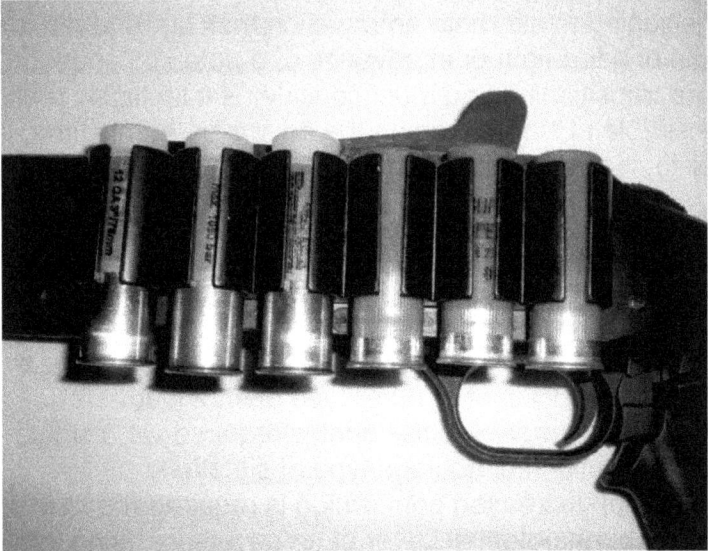

- Hold the shotgun in the strong hand.
- Retrieve a shell or slug from your ammunition source (side-mounted, butt-mounted, belt-mounted or pocket).
- Bring the shell under the receiver and at a point just forward of the trigger guard loading port.

Shotgun Reloading

- Insert the shell forward into the tubular magazine using your thumb and index finger as a guide, while your thumb pushes the shell into the magazine.
- Continue to repeat the process until you have loaded your desired number of alternative rounds.

Shotgun Reloading

- In a pump action shotgun the support hand then slides the forearm to the rear ejecting the previously chambered round and inserting the alternative round.
- In a semi-automatic shotgun the support hand slides the bolt to the rear ejecting the previously chambered round and inserting the alternative round.

Shotgun Reloading

Malfunctions

Failures to Fire and Misfires for Semi-Autos

Failures to Fire or Weapons malfunctions typically fall into one of two categories; either weapons issues or ammunition issues. Weapons issues are often uncontrollable during a fire-fight or tactical engagement. Ammunition problems however may often be addressed during a fire-fight or tactical engagement.

Weapons Failures or Malfunctions are often mechanical problems beyond the shooter's control. Ammunition problems with small arms typically fall into three categories:

- Failure to Fire – comes as the result of a click instead of a bang usually associated with a bad or dud round. Corrective action:
  -First aggressively pump the action to the rear while tilting the shotgun to the right to allow the malfunctioning shell to eject.
  -With a semi-automatic weapon pull the bolt handle back aggressively.
  -Closing of the subsequent action on either the semi-auto or pump should chamber a new round and allow you to return to the fight.
- Failure to Eject – this comes as a result of the expended rounds failure to eject. It may be trapped in the ejection port or sticking out of it (stove pipe). The trigger may be inoperable. With a pump action shotgun you will be unable to close the forearm because of the malfunctioning shell. Corrective action:
  -Kneel and/or get behind cover if possible. If no cover

Shotgun Reloading

is available try and create distance.

-For the Pump Action Shotgun or Semi-Automatic Weapon pull the forearm or bolt back aggressively as you rotate the weapon ejection port down.

-Failures to Eject are often caused by damaged case rims or by worn extractors or ejectors.

- Failure to Feed – comes as the result of the shell in a tubular magazine will jump past the latch that holds it in place. This ties up the action and prevents the forearm from being cycled. In a semi-automatic shotgun it is often caused by an over-expanded shell in the chamber. Corrective action:

-For Pump Action Shotgun's drop to a knee.

-Slam the butt of the shotgun on the ground while you simultaneously pump the action. This should clear the failure to eject. This should only be done in an emergency as it is extremely hard on the shotgun.

-For the Semi-Automatic Shotgun drop to a knee pull the bolt back aggressively while tilting the weapon to the side. This allows you to utilize gravity to assist you in expelling the spent round.

-You may reengage from the kneeling position or come up from an underarm position as it allows you to get back in fight a split second quicker than shouldering the weapon.

Chapter 7
Engaging the Threat

You don't have to die today, but you need to comply!

Engaging the Threat

Fighting in and around your House

Fighting in and around your house can take on many forms depending on your objective. Combing clarity of objective and the subsequent tactical execution is essential to helping you survive the encounter.

Below are some of the more common tactical approaches one may consider:

- Holding your Position
- Taking Ground
- Tactical Escape
- Search and Neutralize

Engaging the Threat

Holding your Position - This is the most common home defense scenario. Despite the initial anxiety, time and the element of surprise is on your side. I*t is your house* or pre-established location and *you have a plan.* You have no immediate need to engage your adversary and no reason to search for them; you actually let them come to you. You have established a position of strength or situational advantage, and have effectively made use of cover or concealment. Point your muzzle at the predetermined approach area and wait to ambush your adversary.

Engaging the Threat

You may or may not choose to warn your adversary; that decision may be dependent on the tactical situation, your defense capabilities and/or legal considerations.

Taking Ground - This involves attacking your attackers. An example may be a rescue of family or team member. This is similar to a hostage rescue. This involves moving rapidly and/or stealthily to close on your adversaries and neutralize the threat often through a precise application of lethal force at close range. The urgency of the situation may determine whether you negotiate, try to de-escalate or give the adversary advanced warning.

In this scenario you typically look to locate your adversary, close the gap and neutralize the threat to save innocent lives.

Engaging the Threat

In some cases this may take the form of seizing a building, room or area of land to be used to hold a position until help arrives or you are able to execute a tactical escape.

Tactical Escape – This involves traveling through a potentially hostile area where there may or may not be adversaries. The objective is not to engage, but rather to escape. An engagement may potentially occur as the result of the hostile impeding your escape. You, your family members or protectees may move rapidly or slowly and stealth like through the projected threat area. There may be no time or desire to attempt to search and neutralize. As you execute your escape your muzzle covers any potentially dangerous areas. You are also slicing the pie as appropriate. The goal is to escape...but in a controlled manner from a position of

Engaging the Threat

strength. A tactical escape beats a tactical encounter every time!

Search and Neutralize - this is probably the least desirable of all the options, as it is essentially a hunt for the adversary. This scenario is most identified with SWAT or Special Forces room clearing. This technique should only be executed by trained professionals or a last option. Because enemies, hostages, civilians, and fellow operators can be closely intermingled, this assault requires a precise application of force. This involves moving cautiously and deliberately through an area in search for an adversary.

Engaging the Threat

The adversary may be hidden (prepared to fight or not) or totally unaware of your presence. With specialized units it often involves violence of action or controlled aggression by the dynamic entry team in order to gain and maintain the physical, psychological and tactical advantage.

Engaging the Threat

Regardless of the particular strategy you employ each will require an understanding of the architectural features of the building involved, the appropriate tactics and how to negotiate them, the cadence of your movements, the ability to identify danger areas and potential threats, and the ability to adopt diverse fighting platforms consistent with the situation and the environment.

Whether you are operating alone, with your family, a partner, or as a member of a team you must be clear on your objective and tactics.

Keys to Surviving a Fire-Fight or Tactical Engagement

Alertness + Anticipation + Distance + Time = Enhances Survival

The ability to stay alert and anticipate situations often gives us the ability to create distance, which buys critical time. Time increases our ability to execute a tactical escape or place a better quality shot; both of which significantly enhance our ability to survive an encounter.

Engaging the Threat

Dealing with Multiple Adversaries

Over 50% of the time we will face more than one adversary. Dealing with multiple adversaries is never at the top of anyone's to do list. Staying alert and avoiding a bad situation should always be the preferred option.

Below are some tactical considerations for dealing with multiple adversaries:

- Try to execute a tactical escape.
- If a tactical escape is not available you must try to stack the engagement in your favor.
- Try to engage the adversaries from behind cover or concealment. Cover has ballistic stopping capabilities. Concealment can't stop a bullet, but can at least hide you from the threats view. If it is harder to see you it is typically harder to hit you:
  -Proactive movement - This may come as a surprise counter attack. For example you are home and undetected by your adversaries and are able to move to a safe position before launching your countermeasures.
  -Reactive movement – This may occur when you have been detected or singled out and your movement was required to improve your defensive or offensive position.
- The first threat you engage should be the one who has the greatest ability to harm or kill you. The ability to harm you is often tied to the adversaries' focus, not merely weapon type or proximity.

Engaging the Threat

Engaging the Threat

Engaging the Threat

- Top picture on the previous page shows your initial position. Tactically this is a very bad place, when engaging multiple adversaries. You are standing abreast of three bad people and each has the ability to orient their weapon toward you unimpeded.
- If you have the ability to control the tempo of the events, at minimum you must try move to cover.
- The second photo shows your preferred position, using your adversaries and the barrel to provide you a split second of cover as you engage the three bad guys.
- Your goal is to line up your adversaries for faster muzzle transition and follow up shots.
- You should attempt to get a least one shot on or in the direction of all of the bad guys as opposed to double or triple tapping one bad guy because his friends will not stop shooting or trying to harm you during the fight.
- If you are a tactical team or family with multiple armed members, decide who will engage whom. This enhances efficiency in dealing with the threat.
  -consider non verbal signals or
  -low whispers
- If the other family members are not trained a practical option may be allowing the trained family member to provide suppression fire while others take cover or attempt escape.

Engaging the Threat

Engaging Threats on the Move

- If the target is moving faster than you, then you must lead the target. Your point of aim should be slightly ahead of your intended point of impact (the target will typically move through the shot pattern).
- If you are moving faster than the target, you must trail the target. Your point of aim will be slightly behind your intended point of impact (the shot string or shot pattern will catch up with the target).
- If the threat is moving directly toward you or directly away from you, you can align your shot directly at the threat without leading or trailing the shot.
- When moving your muzzle between multiple threats you must learn to move your muzzle on the recoil as you line up your next shot.
- Allow your eyes to move to where the adversaries are, however your cheek should stay down on the comb/stock to allow you to break your next shot faster.

Engaging the Threat

Engaging the Threat

Transitioning Shoulders/Hands with your Shotgun

Transitioning shoulders with your shotgun is designed to optimize your ability to take advantage of the available cover or, to get off the line of attack and still make quality hits without getting crossed up or overexposing yourself to the threat.

Firing from the Right Shoulder to the Left Shoulder Moving to the Left

- Mount the shotgun to your shoulder (firing from the right shoulder).
- Focus on the front sight or front sight assembly only for close quarter engagements.
- Squeeze (don't jerk) the trigger
- Transition your hand position by moving your left hand back to the pistol grip and your right hand forward on the fore grip.
- Push the weapon system forward, rocking the butt stock up and over your sling thereby transitioning the weapon to your left shoulder.
- The squarer you keep your body and the stiller you keep your head, the easier it is to maintain a consistent cheek weld from either shoulder.

Engaging the Threat

Engaging the Threat

Engaging the Threat

Tactical Movement and the use of Cover

What is the difference between cover and concealment?
Cover has ballistic stopping capabilities. Brick walls, engine
blocks, very large trees are examples of cover.
Concealment can't stop a bullet, but can hide you from the
threat's view. If it is harder to see you it is harder to hit you.
Drywall, upholstered furniture, hedges, car doors, and side
walls are examples of concealment.

Keys to using cover or concealment:

- Try to stay at least 5 - 6 feet back from your cover.
- This may allow ricochets to go around or over you
  and not into you.
- This will also reduce the possibility of injury from
  shattered debris.
- Allow your shooting platform to match your cover.

Engaging the Threat

Prone Position from Cover

If all you have is a 2 foot high fallen log or rock to hide behind, consider a prone position as your firing platform. *Be very careful when considering a prone position on hard surfaces as bullets may skip into your vitals* (head and chest cavity)!

Engaging the Threat

Kneeling Position from Cover

If all you have is a 3 foot high brick wall or large rock to hide behind consider a kneeling position as your firing platform.

Engaging the Threat

Standing Position from Cover

If all you have is a very solid vertical structure, tree or door to cover or conceal, consider a standing position as your firing platform. Make sure your body position aligns with the cover.

Engaging the Threat

Cover and/or movement are often the two major keys to surviving an attack. There is truth to the old adage, "A moving target is harder to hit." Numerous law enforcement and civilian encounters, as well as force on force training, have shown that people who move off the line of attack significantly increase their ability to survive a firearm or edged weapon encounter.

Engaging the Threat

Keys to using Movement (particularly in close quarters)

During an actual attack

- Get off the line of attack.
- People tend the engage you where you were, not where you are now!
- Movement can often compensate for bad marksmanship. However, a fast mount and great marksmanship often can't compensate for lack of movement.
- If you cannot move after your first shot, try to move after the conclusion of the first encounter.
- Like a boxer, your ability to bob or weave is crucial. Our movement in relation to the face of a clock is our version of bobbing and weaving. Often you can't move totally out of the ring, but you can move off the line of attack.

- Consider moving to 9, 10, 11, 1, 2, 3, 8, 7, 5, or 4 o'clock.
- Avoid moving straight back to 6 o'clock; most bad guys can run forward faster than you can run

Engaging the Threat

backwards. It is too easy to get over run or taken down.
- If your adversary has a firearm, you have not moved out of his or her sight picture!

During a Dynamic Entry or Exit

- Try to alter your standard shooting platform as little as possible.
- The shotgun is typically mounted on the shoulder or underarm to allow for quick acquisition.
- The muzzle is typically below eye level to allow you to see over the muzzle.
- If moving with a team in a line, the weapon will typically be in a low ready position to minimize covering a team member with your weapon.
- Keep your walking gate as consistent as possible:
-If you need to close the gap quicker, take longer strides.
-If you need to slow down closing the gap, take shorter steps.
- Consider bending your knees a little more and incorporate a slight forward lean to aid in absorbing recoil.
- In a dynamic entry or exit, you cannot move any faster than your ability to deliver quality hits on your adversary.

Engaging the Threat

Searching for an Intruder

- Always use a trained partner if and when available
- Wear body armor if available
- Utilize or be conscious of cover
- Do not turn your back on un-cleared areas
- Practice good light discipline
- Practice safe weapons handling
- Use ear pieces to silence radios
- Keep radio traffic to a minimum
- Move quietly and cautiously
- Communicate your observations to your partner
- Cover each other when clearing dark areas and doors

Engaging the Threat

Slicing the Pie (Cornering Techniques)

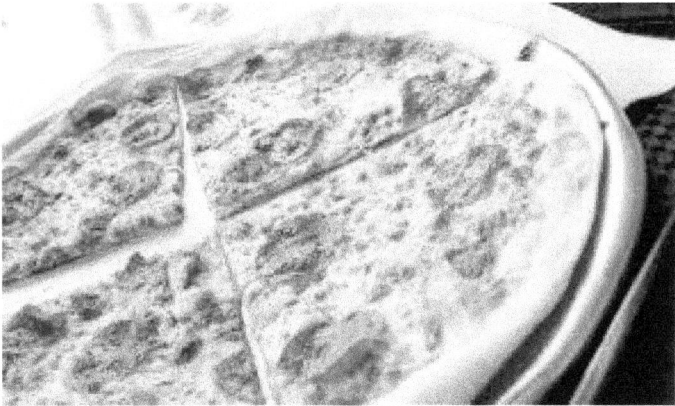

While it is understood that the layout of building and rooms may vary; the basic clearing techniques are pretty standard. Clearing a room or corner is like eating a pizza pie and best done:

- Slowly
- One slice at a time
- In small bites

"Slicing the pie" is a common tactical technique for negotiating corners and objects from a position of cover or concealment and tactical advantage.

As you approach the corner, start as close to the wall as possible without scraping up against it and compromising your position. Your eyes scan the corner vertically from the floor to ceiling, as threats may manifest themselves at various levels.

Engaging the Threat

The further you stay off the corner the greater your visibility will be around the corner. Ultimately your pivot point will be the apex of the corner.

Take a small controlled step 90° away from the wall. This is the start of a semi-circle you will make around the corner. Keep your elbows in and your front foot parallel to your line of sight so that neither will give you away.

The weapon is mounted on your shoulder or in an underarm assault position for extreme close quarter engagements. If you are proficient with engaging from both shoulders the weapon is mounted on the shoulder which allows you to maximize your use of cover.

Engaging the Threat

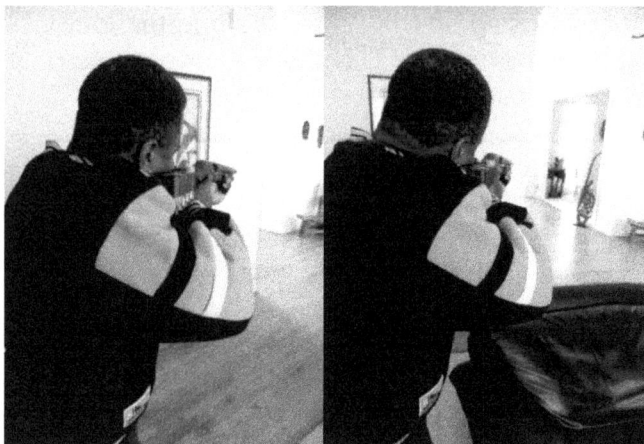

As you continue to move in small 90° increments around the corner your head stays on a swivel. Your body position will be leaning slightly toward the direction you are stepping to allow your head, eyes and the muzzle of your shotgun to see around the corner in small sections at a time. This will allow you to see the potential adversary before he can see you. The muzzle of your shotgun should always point in the direction your eyes are looking this allows you to respond to threats much quicker.

Avoid crossing your feet as this will create on unstable engagement platform. Continue traversing the corner until you have cleared it.

A great practice technique is to get two flashlights and a friend and work on the concepts. As soon as one of you sees any part of the other, shine your flashlight on them. In a short period of time you will have the technique mastered.

Engaging the Threat

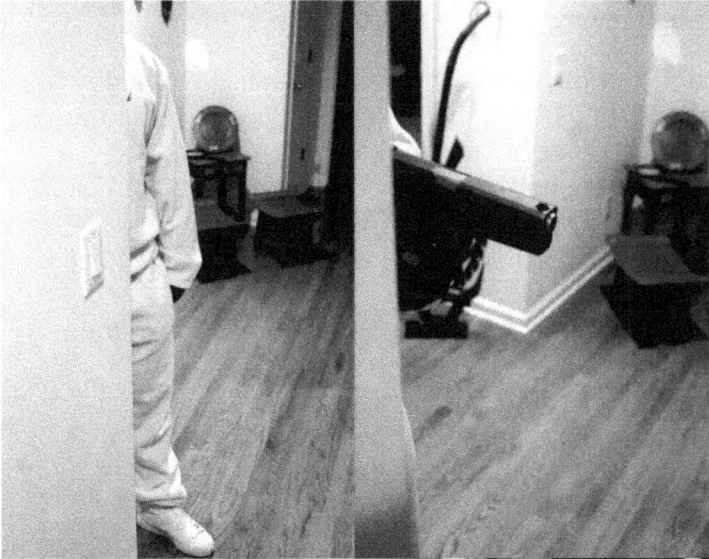

Engaging the Threat

The previous photos represent three different scenarios of what might be waiting for you around the corner:

- In the first photo we don't know whether the bad guy has a weapon, but slicing the pie and staying wide allows you to see the corner of his shoulder.
- In the second photo the bad guy makes another mistake in exposing his weapon beyond the cover.
- In the third and fourth photos we see the bad guy is armed with a knife.
- Just because they are criminals, it doesn't make them tactically smart.
- Make sure your muzzle does not extend beyond the cover and compromise your position as you take a corner.

Engaging the Threat

Clearing Stairs

Clearing or searches which involve stairs can be extremely dangerous, as they force you to potentially expose portions of your body without the ability to lead with your shotgun. When forced to consider clearing steps or escalators make sure that is your only option. Use a partner if available.

Negotiate the area by clearing visible portions which allow you to lead with your shotgun utilizing the slicing the pie techniques. The concepts are they same stairs they just incorporate awkward footing and the need to clear both the horizontal and vertical planes often simultaneously. Consider separating steps or escalators into upper and lower to minimize your exposure.

Engaging the Threat

Confronting an Intruder

- It's recommended to confront an intruder from behind cover
- Maintain maximum distance and get verbal compliance before approaching
- Be alert for a possible second intruder
- Watch the hands for suspected weapons
- Have the suspect interlock his fingers behind his head
- Have the suspect assume a kneeling position and cross his ankles
- If necessary have the suspect go to a prone position with arms extended and hands pointing up
- If the people confronting the intruder are law enforcement or security, one partner covers while the other cuffs the suspect
- Always cuff before searching
- Communicate your status to the response team

Engaging the Threat

Perpetrator/Intruder Down

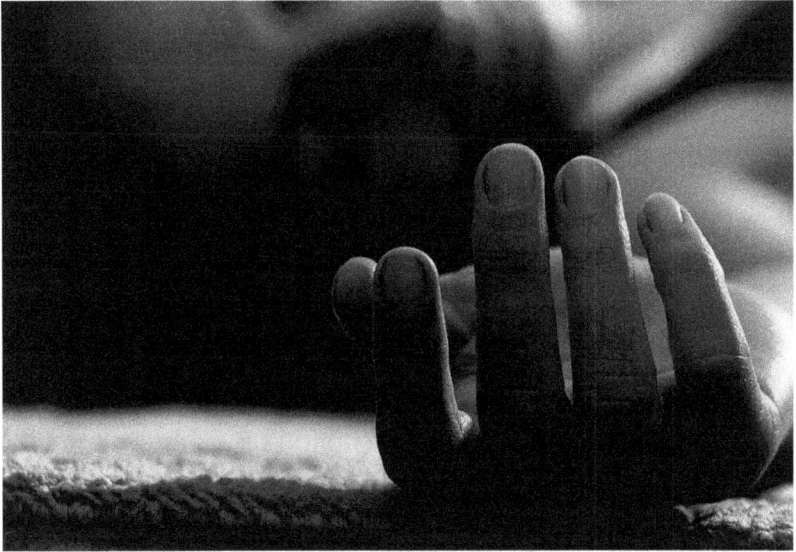

Managing the stress and adrenaline dump of a deadly force encounter require a great amount of self-control. However, the steps you take after a deadly force encounter are as important as the preparation which allowed you to survive.

Most states prohibit the use of force greater than the force being used against you, and when that force ceases so must yours. If you have made the decision to use deadly force you must have felt your life; that of a family member or a third party was in serious danger.

Engaging the Threat

While the legalities of using deadly force will be determined by a judge, here are some important considerations:

- When the perpetrator is no longer a threat stop shooting.
- While you call the authorities continue to check your surroundings, particularly behind you, to make sure the threat has no bad guy buddies attempting a sneak attack.
- Call 911 or ask someone to call the authorities immediately. Ask the dispatcher to send the police. If anyone has been injured also notify them to send an ambulance. Even if you believe the perpetrator may be fatally injured request an ambulance. Give the dispatcher a good description of yourself so police may recognize you.
- Now call your attorney. First call is to 911, second call is to your attorney!
- Don't misrepresent the facts to anyone, especially the dispatcher or police. Do not alter evidence at the scene. If you alter evidence eventually it will be found out. Your credibility will be lost and you may face charges.
- Secure the weapon. If the perpetrator has a weapon, try to secure the weapon. This does not necessarily mean picking it up. You may accomplish this by merely instructing the perpetrator to move away from the weapon. There may be times when you have to literally secure the weapon for your own safety or the safety of others. If this is the case and you must pick it up, consider sticking an ink pen in the muzzle/barrel and picking it up. Other times you may secure the

Engaging the Threat

weapon by slightly moving it away from the perpetrator's grasp with your foot.

- If you are providing executive protection, have one of the other agents get your client out of harm's way while you remain available for the police.
- If a crowd appears and starts to become riotous and you no longer feel safe, immediately tell the dispatcher if they are still on the telephone or redial the police as you head straight to the police station.
- As soon as it is tactically possible secure your own weapon. You don't want to be standing with a gun in your hand when the police arrive. There will be times that you may have to hold a perpetrator at bay until the police arrive. If that is the case and the police say, "Put your gun down," please heed that advice. You don't want to become an accidental shooting because you were mistaken for the perpetrator!
- There is a good chance you will be handcuffed or arrested even in a self-defense shooting, until the police can sort out the situation. The police are also concerned for their own safety and since one person is already down, they don't want the second person down to be them.

Engaging the Threat

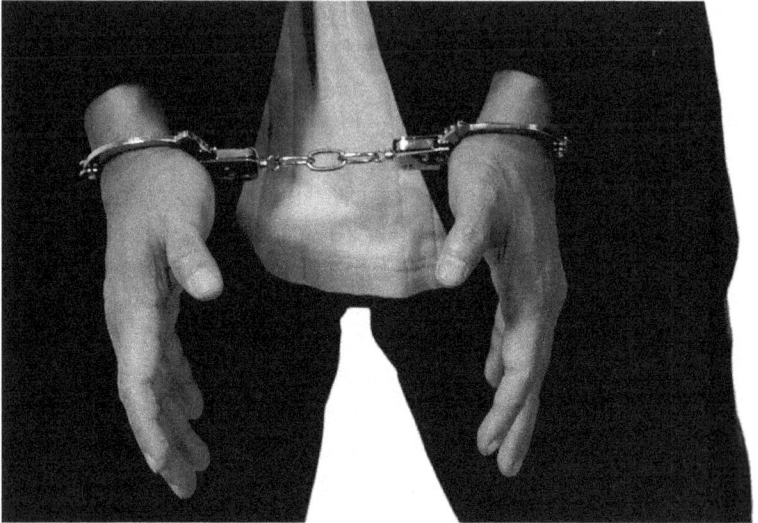

- Tell the police you would like to press charges or file a complaint against the perpetrator. Point out any witnesses on the scene or relevant evidence the police should be aware of.
- Don't talk to anyone about the case until it has been adjudicated. If you are arrested and placed in a holding cell, avoid talking to anyone about your situation. You never know who may be trying to cut their own deal. Don't talk to your family, friends, co-workers or strangers about the case. People will try and press you for details. Just advise them, "Unfortunately this is still an ongoing investigation and I am not at liberty to make any comments." While you may not be charged criminally in the case, it doesn't mean you may not become the party of a civil suit.

Engaging the Threat

Weapon Retention

The primary rule in weapon retention is to stay alert. Maintaining a safe distance from a potential threat is a key component of weapon retention. Awareness is often the key to not becoming a victim. It is important to understand that your gun may not be the only thing the attacker is looking to take from you.

Key considerations in weapons retention:

- Awareness is always our first defense. Be aware of who is around you.
- If someone grabs for your shotgun, be aware that they may be prepared to kill you. You must be prepared to react immediately.
- If you believe their intent is deadly force, you must be more motivated than they are to protect your weapon and most importantly your life.
- Your options are many but most importantly you must be committed to the fight!

Engaging the Threat

Countermeasures

- If someone grabs the muzzle of your shotgun, avoid getting into a tug of war. Simply get the muzzle back on them, and discharge your weapon.

Engaging the Threat

- This often may be achieved while standing or by dropping to a knee and firing your weapon the bad guy will probably let go!
- If the bad guy happens to take your weapon and you carry an alternative weapon (handgun or knife), transition to your alternate weapon and handle your business.
- If you don't have alternate weapons employ your specific close quarter countermeasures (hands, fists, elbows, knees, flashlight, baton, pepper spray etc.). You must attack the attacker. To protect your life you must be more motivated than the threat. For some you may feel not fighting back is your best option.

Engaging the Threat

Non-shootable Threat

Just because you have a weapon, all situations don't
necessarily call for discharging it. For non-shootable
adversaries the shotgun may be used as an impact weapon.
If your weapon is to be used as an impact weapon, your
finger must be outside of the trigger guard to avoid an
accidental discharge.

Muzzle Thrust

Engaging the Threat

- While holding the shotgun your strong hand should be positioned on the shotgun wrist with your finger outside of the trigger guard and indexed along the side of the frame. The support hand is positioned on the forearm. Thrust the muzzle of the shotgun into either:
  -Solar plexus
  -Groin
  -Chin or face
- Make sure you step into the move and avoid an arms only thrust.

Engaging the Threat

Receiver Thrust

- While holding the shotgun (strong hand on the shotgun wrist, support hand on the forearm) thrust the receiver into the solar plexus.
- Make sure you step into the move...avoid an arms only thrust).

Engaging the Threat

Butt Thrust

- While holding the shotgun (strong hand on the shotgun wrist, support hand on the forearm) thrust the butt of the shotgun into:
  -Solar plexus
  -Groin
  -Chin or face
- Make sure you step into the move…avoid an arms only thrust.

Engaging the Threat

High Butt Thrust

- An alternate move on the butt thrust is to step into your adversary on a 90 degree move, thrusting the toe of the butt into your adversary's ribs or chin.
- When striking to the chin, this move may come from a horizontal or vertical toe position.

Engaging the Threat

Shotgun Disarming

Engaging the Threat

Shotgun Disarming Explained

- As the assailant presents his shotgun at you, try and de-escalate the situation.
- Two critical components of a successful disarm are to come from a non-threatening posture and attacking the attacker.
- The first part of the disarm starts with surrendering either real or faux, with your hands at weapon height.
- As you fain compliance, simultaneously turn off the line of attack, and divert the muzzle away from you with your hand or forearm.
- Once you get the muzzle off you, keep the muzzle off you. Execute a low line attack, with the ball of your foot strike directly onto the front or side of the kneecap executing a hyper-extension or knee break.
- Follow up with a palm heel strike to temple or button of the nose or fingers to the attacker's eyes.
- After you have caused the attacker extreme pain then execute the disarm.
- It is much easier to execute a disarm if the attacker is no longer at 100% of their capabilities.

Engaging the Threat

Negotiating Darkness

Engaging the Threat

Keep in mind that over 70% of encounters will occur at night or in low light conditions. Most criminals prefer night as they feel they have a greater opportunity to move in the cover of darkness and potentially avoid detection. In low light conditions it is important to remain calm. Your movements are often slow and methodical unless executing a rapid/dynamic entry or exit maneuver. Often when one sense is taken away the other senses become heightened. Allow those senses to work for you as you plan your search or exit. Be conscious of:

- Noise - to help you locate a threat or potential adversary
- Smell - use your nose to help you detect a potential threat or adversary
  -body odor
  -cologne or perfume
  -smoke cigarette or tobacco
  -any smells uncommon to your environment

Engaging the Threat

It is often more beneficial to stay put and behind cover let your adversary come to you if an immediate escape is not available to you. The major reason for a light is not to see the sights on your shotgun, but to identify a potential adversary and provide you positive target acquisition. This allows you to better scan the environment and when a potential threat is located better scan their body or bodies for potential weapons or monitor their movements.

There are a multitude of light configurations which can be attached to you shotgun. They range from integrated operating systems (light embedded in the forearm or vertical grips); to bracket attachments which often attach to the ammunition tube for a flash lights, to at it simplest option holding a traditional hand held light in your support hand

Engaging the Threat

along the side of the forearm of the shotgun. They may be operated by on/off buttons mounted on the side or rear of the light source to pressure switches.

The light sources may often be standard white, halogen, green or strobe lights. Strobe lights often make it harder for a threat or adversary to pin down your particular position within the illuminated area. Those same lights may also make it harder for you to detect minor movements on a potential threat.

Please keep in mind once you illuminate an area your position will be compromised. Some considerations when utilizing a light:

- In defensive or tactical situations you should avoid using a light unless or until absolutely necessary.
- Consider using short bursts of lights 1 – 2 seconds on then off as you scan and area, if no threat is detected, with the light off move to a new location before turning it on again.
- Move low and slow.
- Angle the beam of light at the ceiling as this allows the light to reflect off the ceiling and illuminate more of the room.
- If working with a team member or family member, keep a little distance between yourselves; making it harder for the adversary to line you up.
- If a potential threat is detected, remember scan the body with particular focus on the hands and feet as they have the ability to be used most quickly in a threatening or harmful manner.

Engaging the Threat

- If your partner stays or moves outside of the light beam he or she will often remain almost invisible to the potential threat.
- The person holding the light should keep it pointed in the direction of the potential threat. All team or family members should also remain alert to other sounds or possible movements as the potential threat may not be alone. Remember to be conscious of what is potentially behind you (check your six).

In low light situations the potential threat or adversary has four major options:

- Stay hidden if they have not been detected.
- Choose to fight.
- Choose to flee.
- Choose to comply with your commands.

Please be very conscious that once you light an area you have compromised your position. Since the threat now realizes you are there may consider any of the above once you turn the light off to move again. You need to remain mentally and physically prepared to deal with any of the above options.

Below are some of the more common used shotgun light companies:

- Insight Technologies
- LaserMax
- Streamlight
- Surefire

Engaging the Threat

Chapter 8

One Hand Operation

"Everybody has a fight plan until they get punched in the mouth!"
Mike Tyson, Former Heavyweight Boxing Champ

One Hand Operation

Injured Operator - One Hand Operation

Mike Tyson once said, "Everybody has a fight plan until they get punched in the mouth." While very admirable we would love to think because of our superior training we will never be injured during an encounter. For those who are veterans of multiple encounters, the reality is there is a good chance we may be injured or at minimum be forced to use our other hand for other activities (i.e. moving another person out of the way, carrying something or someone).

The most difficult challenge in manipulating your shotgun with one hand will typically be the weight of the weapon. However in a real fire-fight your adrenaline, willingness to survive or protect your family will probably give you the added strength, to perform the operations.

Activating the Pump Shotgun

- Your first consideration should be to move to cover or at minimum create distance from your adversary.
- Second with your non injured or non occupied hand grasp your shotgun by the forearm and allow gravity to assist you in cycling the action.
- If you don't have the strength to cycle the action without support, drop to a knee and allow the ground to provide you a firm base in which to cycle the action.
- In the photos on the next page, I am allowing the railroad ties to provide the support to cycle the action before returning back to fire control.

One Hand Operation

Activating the Pump Shotgun

One Hand Operation

Loading the Shotgun While Injured

One Hand Operation

Whether the shotgun is a pump or semi-automatic:

- Try to work from cover if possible or at minimum try to create distance until you can get back into the fight.
- Place the shotgun between your knees.
- The muzzle pointed toward the ground.
- The sights pointing down/loading port up.
- Reach down and wrap your arm around the stock for stability to help brace the shotgun while reloading.
- Load the shotgun as usual through the tubular magazine with the non injured arm/hand.
- Eyes remained focused on the threat or adversary.
- Activate the action release or cycle the action with your non injured or non occupied arm.
- An alternate method of cycling the action with the semi-automatic shotgun is to use your belt loop to activate the action lever.
- With the pump shotgun allow either gravity or the ground to assist you in cycling the action.
- Eyes remained focused on the threat or adversary.

One Hand Operation

Getting Back into the Fight

Handling your Business

- Your initial move was to seek cover if available.
- If no cover was available you created distance to make your adversary have a more difficult shot.

One Hand Operation

- You either allowed gravity to assist you in cycling the action on your pump or you placed your semi-automatic between your knees and cycled the action.
- With the shotgun still between your knees you loaded your ammunition.
- Now it is time to get back in fight.
- Remember you may fire from a standing, kneeling or prone position.
- The most important thing is to stay in the fight if a tactical escape has not presented itself to you.
- Throughout the engagement your eyes have stayed focused on the threat or adversary.
- You may have incorporated your belt, ammunition belt or tee-shirt to make an impromptu sling if required.

One Hand Operation

Alternate Tactic for Injured Operators (Weapon Transition)

One Hand Operation

Some considerations for transitioning to an alternate weapon:

- The shotgun is damaged.
- The shotgun is too heavy for you to manage with one hand.
- You are out of or extremely low on shotgun ammunition.
- You are about to get into an extreme close quarter engagement and weapon retention is a concern. Transitioning to your secondary creates additional separation between you and your adversary.
- Employing a two-point or three-point sling allows you drop your primary weapon and transition to your secondary more efficiently.
- With a single-point you can enhance the stability during the transition by flipping the toe of the shotgun butt-stock under the sling.
- Whatever your reason for transitioning your eyes should stay threat focused throughout the engagement.

One Hand Operation

Injured Operator Technique with a Vertical Foregrip

One Hand Operation

Injured Operator Technique Vertical Foregrip Explain

- While engaging the adversary if you are hit with a round in your reaction hand and you lose the functionality of that limb.
- In order to activate the pump and remain on fire control (weapon pointed at adversary and ready to fire), drop to a knee and allow the inside of your thigh to cycle the action to eject the spent shell (photo 2).
- Then use the outside of your thigh as a brace against the inside of the vertical grip to close the action and chamber a new shell (photo 3).
- You can then take a real-time shot from a kneeling position (photo 4) or you can return to a standing position and engage the threat with one hand as indicated in the photo on the following page.

One Hand Operation

Chapter 8

Shotgun Accessories

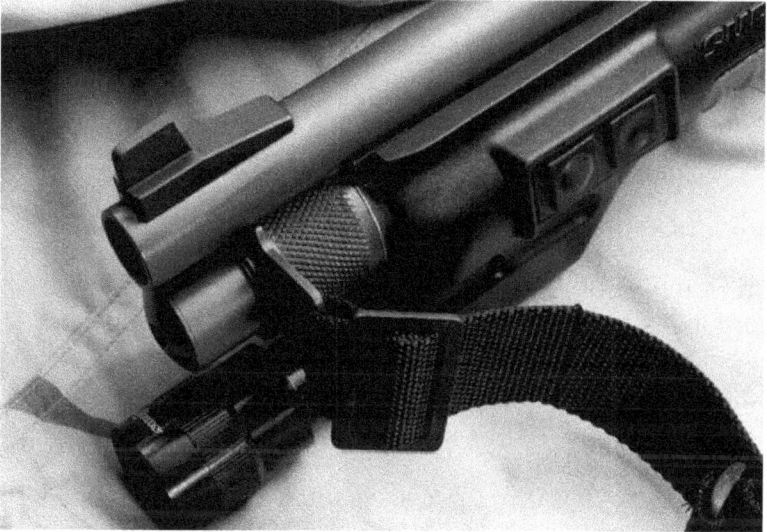

If your accessories don't help you fight more efficiently you don't need them.

Shotgun Accessories

There are a number of accessories which one can consider for your defensive or tactical shotgun. One of the most important considerations is to keep your shotgun as functionally simple as possible. Any high-tech modifications should not come at the expense of simplicity. The modifications should help make your shotgun easier to operate. If you are considering any high-tech modifications you must also ask yourself: Can I still operate the shotgun effectively if the high-tech devices fail or malfunction? Throughout the years one of the things that has always made the shotgun an effective tool was its ease of operation in the face of danger.

Butt Pads

Butt Pads – One of the most important considerations for all shotguns is a good butt-pad. Butt-pads are essential to keeping the shotgun from slipping particularly once the shotgun has been mounted. The last thing you want during a tactical engagement is your shotgun slipping out of the shoulder pocket.

Shotgun Accessories

The choice of enhanced recoil reduction or not is a matter of preference. There are a number of good choices in recoil pads on the market and Limbsaver and Hogue are two of the best at reducing recoil.

Knoxx Spec Ops Recoil System – highly recommended for reducing recoil. Significantly reduces recoil and muzzle flip and aids in helping you get your follow up shots on target faster.

Shotgun Accessories

Slings

Shotgun slings help reduce fatigue for operators who have to carry a shotgun for extended periods of time or make weapons transition easier. There are a number of sling options from single point, three-point, to ammunition carrying slings. Below are some of the more commonly used ones.

ASP, Blackhawk, Galco, Magpul, Viking Tactics and Vickers Combat (Blue Force Gear) and 511 are just a few of the more common manufacturers. Regardless of the manufacturer, what is highly recommended is a sling with quick detach capabilities and adjust on the fly options which will allow you to work from a number of shooting platforms, and multi-mission considerations. My primary consideration for a sling is to enhance (not limit) my fighting capabilities. Carry positions for comfort are a secondary concern as there is nothing comfortable about home invasions or CQB.

Shotgun Accessories

Single Point Sling

Single point slings – a single-point sling is a single loop which goes around the shooter's body, over one and under the other shoulder. It connects to the weapon near the stock to receiver junction. The single-point sling provides minimal support for carrying the Shotgun, but provides maximum range of motion when the Shotgun is in use. A single-point sling allows shooting from any position without the shooter extricating them from the sling.

Shotgun Accessories

When transitioning to a secondary weapon, the shotgun simply hangs from the single connection point. This provides minimal control of the shotgun during movement and is generally not the most preferred carry position for movement over extended distances. You can however reduce the actual movement of the weapon if you tuck the toe of the butt-stock underneath the sling.

Shotgun Accessories

Two Point Slings

Two point slings – is a sling which connects to the front and rear of the shotgun, similar to the old loop slings. Some modern two-point slings may use sling mounts on the side of the weapon instead of the bottom, to facilitate carry of shotguns with high-capacity box magazines (i.e. Saiga shotguns). Two-point slings provide more control over the weapon when slung than the single-point, and they can be used in all the carry positions as the original loop slings.

Shotgun Accessories

The primary limitations of conventional two-point slings were they were not adjustable on the fly, and weapons transition typically meant extracting yourself from the sling to perform those types of movements. The modern modified two-point slings can be attached to the rifle in different places. The rear attachment point can be at the rear of the stock or at the stock to receiver junction; the front attachment point can be near the front sight base or nearer to the receiver. This flexibility allows the shooter to set it up for maximum freedom of movement as well as control of the shotgun.

Shotgun Accessories

Three point slings – the three-point sling, which connects to the front and rear of the weapon, and has a slider so the loop around the shooter's body connects to the main loop about halfway back from the sling's forward attachment point. Three-point slings provide more control of the shotgun than the other two types, and they allow more carry modes. The primary advantage of the three-point sling is that it maximizes control of the primary weapon when transitioning

Shotgun Accessories

to your secondary weapon. When the weapon is dropped using the three-point sling, it will generally hang diagonally across the front of the body, maintaining good muzzle control. When slung in this position, it is easy to walk, and the gun can be rotated around to the shooter's side or back to get it out of the way. The primary disadvantage of the three point sling is it doesn't provide for easy crossover/shoulder transition.

Shotgun Accessories

Blackhawk Shotgun Sling – helps provide additional ammunition storage and is particularly beneficial on shotguns which aren't equipped with alternate side saddle or butt stock ammunition carriers.

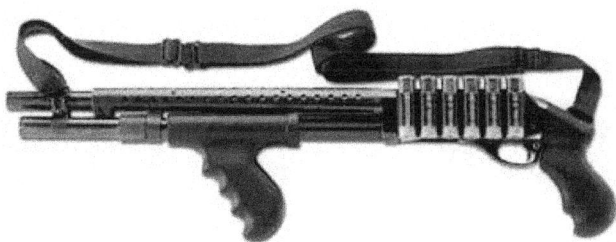

Shotgun Accessories

Foregrips

Vertical Foregrips for Weaver and Picatinny rails or forearm incorporated – help reduce recoil, and muzzle flip and aids in helping get your follow up shots on target quicker. Some vertical grips are also equipped with flashlight adapters.

ERGO Tri Rails   MAKO Three Rail forend

Surefire M69 Picatinny Rail   Hogue

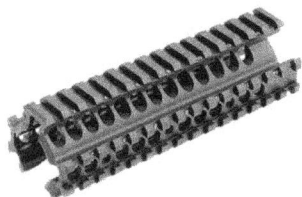

Shotgun Accessories

Combination Foregrips/Weapons Light Systems

Surefire Shotgun forend Weapon Lights

FAB Defense T - Grip Tactical Foregrip - Flashlight Adapter

Shotgun Accessories

Magpul AFG

Magpul RVG

Gear Sector Vertical Grip

FAB Defense Vertical Grip

Blackhawk Rail Mount Vertical

Tapco

214

Shotgun Accessories

Sights

Sights are designed to make visual acquisition or slight alignment easier. Sights may range from beads, to blades, to night sights, to tritium, to ghost rings, to red dots or reflex or holographic sights.   The most important consideration should be: Does the sight I am considering help support the type of use I am preparing to employ this weapon for? Remember the shotgun is historically a close range weapon and most factory installed sights are typically satisfactory for most jobs.

Red Dots – are a common classification for a type of non-magnifying reflector (or reflex) sights for firearms that gives the user an aim-point in the form of an illuminated red dot. A standard design uses a red light-emitting diode (LED) at the focus of collimating optics which generates a dot style illuminated reticle that stays in alignment with the weapon the sight is attached to regardless of eye position (nearly parallax free). They are considered to be fast acquisition and easy to use gun sights for self-defense, target shooting, hunting, and in police and military applications.

Shotgun Accessories

Representative Samples of Common Red Dot Sights

Burris Fastfire III   Aim Point Pro

Aim Point Micro T1   EOTech XPS-2-0   Trijicon RMR

Shotgun Accessories

Bead sights – many shotguns do not have rear sights. Most have a bead at the muzzle end, and a ventilated rib on top of the barrel leading up to the bead. When pointing a shotgun at a target, the rib and front bead should be aligned so that you are looking straight down the barrel, to properly hit the target. If the bead appears to be higher or lower than the rib, then you are not looking straight down the barrel, and the shot will not hit the intended target.

Shotgun Accessories

Trijicon Adjustable Night Sights

HiViz Fiber Optic FS

Truglo Gobble Dot Xtreme

Truglo Slug Series Sights

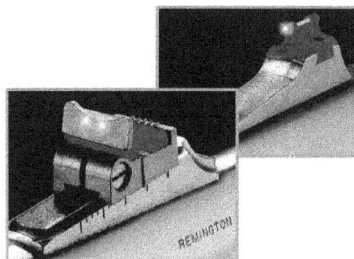

Appendix

Appendix

Frequently Used Firearm Terms

Accuracy – the measure of precision in consistently obtaining a desired result. In shooting, the measure of a bullet's or gun's precision in grouping all shots close to the center of impact.

Action – the mechanism of a firearm by which it is loaded, locked, fired and unloaded. In a revolver, usually means the cylinder. In semi-automatic Shotguns it usually refers to the slide. In rifles, refers to the bolt mechanism.

Automatic Weapon – a firearm is said to be an "automatic weapon" if it is capable of firing more than one cartridge by pressing the trigger.

Barrel – the part of a firearm the bullet passes through before exiting the firearm.

Bench rest – a heavy table or shelf, which a Shotgun or rifle can be fired.

Bore – the inside of the barrel of a gun of any kind.

Bullet – The missile only, becomes a projectile when in flight. Not to be applied to the cartridge.

Caliber – approximately bore or grove diameter expressed (in English) in decimals of an inch, otherwise in the metric system.

Cartridge – a complete unit of ammunition assembled (i.e. case, propellant powder, primer and bullet or shot). Usually only applied to rifle and handgun ammunition, but occasionally to shotgun shot shells.

Appendix

Center Fire (CF) – refers to centrally located primer in the base metallic cartridges. Most center fire cartridges are reloadable.

Chamber – the part of the bore at the breech, formed to accept and support the cartridge, shell or slug.

Clip – a metal device that holds a number of cartridges for fast loading into the magazine of a rifle or Shotgun.

Close quarters combat (CQC) or close quarters battle (CQB) - is a type of fighting in which small units engage the enemy with personal weapons at very short range, potentially to the point of hand-to-hand combat or fighting with hand weapons such as knives. In the typical CQC scenario, the attackers try a very fast, violent takeover of a vehicle or structure controlled by the defenders, who usually have no easy way to withdraw.

Firearm – generally a "gun" carried and used by one person.

Flash Sight Picture – as you raises the weapon to eye level, your point of focus switches from the adversary to the front sight, ensuring that the front and rear sights (when applicable) are in proper alignment left and right, but not necessarily up and down. Pressure is applied to the trigger as the front sight is being acquired, and you break the shot, this image is referred to as the "Flash Sight Picture."

FPS – abbreviation for feet-per-second. Also ft/se, fps or f.p.s.

Grooves – spiral cuts or impressions in the bore of a firearm which cause a bullet to spin as it moves through the barrel.

Appendix

Group – the pattern made at the target of number of shots fired with one aiming point and usually one sight setting. It is measured from center to center of the holes farthest from each other.

Magazine – that portion of a firearm which holds the cartridges in preparation for the bolt, slide or mechanism to feed a cartridge from the magazine into the chamber. Magazines may be fixed as an internal portion of the firearm or removable. They may be square, tubular or round/drum like.

Misfire – complete failure of a cartridge to fire after the primer is struck by the firing pin.

Muzzle – the front end of the barrel. The point at which a projectile or shot leaves the barrel.

Primer – also called "cap," deriving from "percussion cap" which is the priming form used with some muzzle loading arms.

Projectile – a bullet or any other object projected by force and continuing in motion by its own inertia. A bullet is not a projectile until it is in motion.

Recoil – the backward thrust or "kick," of a gun caused by the reaction to the powder gases pushing the bullet or shot shell through the bore and jet effect of the gasses themselves.

Rifling – parallel spiral grooves cut or impressed into the bore of rifles and Shotguns in order to make the bullets spin, insuring steady, and point on flight to the target.

Appendix

Round – a military term meaning one complete cartridge.

Semi-automatic – a firearm that fires one cartridge (and only one cartridge) each time the trigger is pressed. Semi-Automatic firearms eject the empty cartridge, load a fresh cartridge from the magazine, chamber the cartridge and lock the breech automatically.

Sighting In – firing of a weapon to determine its point of impact at a specified range and to adjust the sights so the point of impact matches the sights.

Velocity – the speed at which a projectile travels, it is usually measured in feet per second (fps) at a given range.

Zero – that adjustment of a gun's sight that will place an aimed shot at the desired point of impact at a given range.

Appendix

References

Benelli USA
901 Eight Street
Pocomake, MD 21851
www.benelliusa.com

Blackhawk
6160 Commander Parkway
Norfolk, VA 23502
www.blackhawk.com

ERGO Grips
P.O. Box 1459
Moriarty, NM
www.ergogrips.net

FAB Defense
43 Yakov Olamy Street
Moshav Mishmar Hashiva
50297 Israel
www.fab-defense.com

Gear Sector
P.O. Box 47
Portage, IN 46368
www.gearsector.com

Kel Tec
P.O. Box 236009
Cocoa, FL 32923
www.keltecweapons.com

Appendix

O.F. Mossberg & Sons, Inc.
7 Grasso Ave
North Haven, CT 06473
www.mossberg.com

"On Combat: The Psychology and Physiology of Deadly Conflict in War and in Peace" by Dave Grossman and Loren W. Christensen

Remington Arms, LLC
870 Remington Drive
Madison, NC 27025
www.remington.com

The Mako Group
1 Lenox Ave
Farmingdale, NY 11735
www.themakogroup.com

Wilson Combat
2234 CR 719
Berryville, AR 72616
www.wilsoncombat.com

Appendix

Index

Appendix

Appendix

Appendix

Appendix

Final Note:

I hope you found the book beneficial, and that I was able to provide you some additional information to help you not only improve your tools, but most importantly enhance your tactics to help you harden the target. My goal is not to make you fearless, but to show you how through increased awareness and enhanced training we can make you fear less, and significantly enhance your ability to repel a deadly encounter. When it comes to extreme acts of violence there is only victory and severe injury. May victory always be on the side of you and your family.

"Six"

www.ingramcontent.com/pod-product-compliance
Lightning Source LLC
Chambersburg PA
CBHW061253110426
42742CB00012BA/1900